NO LONGER PROPERTY OF
ANYTHINK LIBRARIES/
RANGEVIEW LIBRARY DISTRICT

simple
stunning
BRIDE

CELEBRATING YOUR STYLE ALL THE WAY TO THE BIG DAY

Karen Bussen

STEWART, TABORI & CHANG • NEW YORK

Published in 2010 by Stewart, Tabori & Chang
An imprint of ABRAMS

Copyright © 2010 by Karen Bussen

Cover photo: © 2010 by Sabine Scherer.
Shot on location at The White Dress by the shore in Clinton, Connecticut.

PHOTO CREDITS:

Jenson Sutta: 1, 31, 54, 60 (right), 76, 123; Virginie Blachère: 2, 51, 62. 72, 96;
Sabine Scherer: 5, 8, 17, 18, 28, 34, 44, 56–57, 58, 59, 60 (left and center), 71, 74, 75, 78, 79, 82 (right),
84, 87, 92, 95, 99, 100, 103, 104, 109, 111, 118, 128; Cappy Hotchkiss: 7, 20, 24, 48, 117;
Mel Barlow: 11, 38, 61; Brian Dorsey: 13, 14, 23, 27, 68, 69, 70, 73, 77, 81, 124; Steve DePino: 66;
Lawrence Jenkins/Nadia Islam: 68; Christian Oth: 82 (left), 91; Belathée: 101, 106, 115; Carla Ten Eyck: 112

All rights reserved. No portion of this book may be reproduced, stored in a retrieval system,
or transmitted in any form or by any means, mechanical, electronic, photocopying, recording,
or otherwise, without written permission from the publisher.

Library of Congress Cataloging-in-Publication Data:
Bussen, Karen.
    Simple stunning bride / Karen Bussen.
        p. cm.
    ISBN 978-1-58479-838-5
    1. Weddings— Planning. 2. Brides. I. Title.
    HQ745.B879 2010
    395.2'2—dc22   2009036225

Editor: Jennifer Levesque
Designer: Susi Oberhelman
Production Manager: Tina Cameron

The text of this book was composed in Helvetica Neue and New Caledonia

Printed and bound in China

10 9 8 7 6 5 4 3 2 1

Stewart, Tabori & Chang books are available at special discounts when purchased in quantity
for premiums and promotions as well as fundraising or educational use. Special editions can also be created
to specification. For details, contact specialsales@abramsbooks.com or the address below.

THE ART OF BOOKS SINCE 1949

115 West 18th Street
New York, NY 10011
www.abramsbooks.com

contents

INTRODUCTION You, as a Bride

"I said to him that I thought he must be aware why I wished him to come here, and that it would make me too happy if he would consent to what I wished (to marry me); we embraced each other over and over again, and he was so kind, so affectionate. Oh to feel I was and am loved by such an angel as Albert was too great a delight to describe . . . I really felt it was the happiest, brightest moment of my life."

—QUEEN VICTORIA

The process of becoming a bride is different for every woman. Some have dreamt about their wedding day for years (I've received e-mails from women who start planning their weddings before even getting engaged!), while others may never have given it any thought at all. Some women know exactly what they want and can't wait to jump right into the thick of designing their celebrations, while others are not so clear about their wedding vision, or they're just less focused on the details. I'm not married, so of course people ask me all the time what my wedding would be like, and you know what I tell them? I have no idea.

Perhaps one of the above scenarios is true for you, perhaps not. But whether you've accepted a proposal or whether, like the legendary, quintessentially modern Queen Victoria, you've made the proposal yourself (at the time, it would have been inappropriate for a man who was not the Queen's royal equal to do the asking), your desire to be married has landed you in the sweetest of clubs—you're a bride-to-be.

Traditionally, brides didn't have all that much to do in preparation for their nuptials, as parents often dealt with most of the details, so the newly engaged woman had more time to enjoy the celebration and to get ready for married life. But things have changed. Brides are now expected (and generally want) to host highly personal festivities, with signature cocktails, sophisticated color stories, elegant menus, handmade details, and clever guest favors—many times while juggling a full-time job, family pressures, and their relationships.

In addition, just as there are countless options and endless decisions to be made about every element of the wedding, every woman's approach to the process is different. That's why those wedding calendars that insist you must do this or that by this date or that date just don't work for everyone. And that's why some brides dream of a modern loft wedding and others envision a classic country club celebration or a wedding on the beach. That's why some plan their weddings in a year, and some in a month.

Despite their differences in approach and personality, I've noticed that there is a commonality that most brides share: It's a desire to delight and please others. They want to make a good impression, to be a gracious hostess, and to be a loving partner throughout the process. They want to be and to express their best self in every way, and at the same time, they're concerned about making sure the celebration reflects their own style and priorities. Does this sound like you?

If it were as easy as just acknowledging that, yes, we'd like everything on this most important day to be perfect, then there would be no need for me to write this book. But what I've noticed in working with and talking to so many brides is that some of the most fabulous, wonderful, accomplished women are putting incredible pressure on themselves to achieve perfection in every area that relates to their wedding.

All the normal things we deal with every day—what to wear, what to serve for dinner, what kind of music to listen to—suddenly become critical elements at "the most important party ever." Personal choices often feel more difficult when they're applied to wedding concerns, and I've observed that it sometimes seems as if the act of donning an engagement ring activates an imaginary meter designed to judge and evaluate a gal's every move and decision.

I've received tearful calls on my cell phone from distressed brides who've just bought a gown and are worried it's not *the one*. Hair and makeup and napkin folds and customized stamps and place settings and bridesmaid shoes have been fretted over and discussed more than you would ever think possible, even by women who don't normally worry about these things.

At a wedding-planning meeting a few years back, one witty groom asked his sweet, if slightly detail-obsessed bride (she really couldn't decide whether or not to offer mini tuna sandwiches along with the bagels at her post-wedding brunch), whether she was about to "take a ride on the crazy train."

I was inspired by that comment to start thinking about this book, and my goal within these pages is to help you identify your own bridal style and organize your process so you can enjoy yourself and stay off that crazy wedding train in favor of a more relaxing trip toward your destination: the big day!

Now, don't get me wrong—the details are important. Thinking and planning in advance will certainly help make things run more smoothly on the big day, and I'm all for it. Heck, I wrote a wedding-planning workbook, and I believe in using tools. But what might surprise you is, I'm not writing this book to tell you how to be the perfect bride. If you're looking for the definitive guide to 1,001 flawless updos or the top 1,000 crunches for your washboard bridal abs, you won't find those topics here.

Why? Well, the fact is there are plenty of books and websites filled with countdowns and mock receiving line dialogues and way too much information about sugar flowers. You can feel pressured to upgrade things you don't even care about, or to hire a videographer you don't like just because your calendar says to wrap up that task at this point in your timeline. Instead, I've decided to tune out the noise and distill the most important information into a book that aims to inspire and guide you to create your own process. I want you to be in control of your priorities, your health, your attitudes, and the details that matter most to you.

Stick with me, lady! I've been there and seen it all, and I'd be delighted to be your guide. I'll be honest about what you need to know, I'll help you enjoy what's fun, and I'll strongly encourage you to dispense with things that just don't matter.

My goal is to give you some great advice from my years of experience with hundreds of weddings, and to inspire you to enjoy every minute of this special time in your life: a time of new beginnings, exciting festivities, and happy moments. I want you to celebrate being you. After all, your fiancé chose you because you are unique and special.

In *Simple Stunning Bride*, I'll outline some of the classic and current bridal responsibilities and traditions, and I'll offer you tips and tricks I've discovered while working with and talking to many, many brides. We'll explore lots of topics, from time management and relationships, to hair and makeup and accessories—and *the dress*. I've also enlisted the help of some amazing industry experts and friends, who will offer you their wedding wisdom. Our aim is to help you focus on feeling good, staying in driver's seat, and enjoying the process.

Speaking of experts, who better to offer advice to those about to wed than those who've already made it down the aisle? In each chapter, and in a special section at the end of the book, you'll find stories, thoughts, and perspective from real brides in a section I call B2B.

Your time preparing to be a bride offers a chance to be pampered, feted, and adored. It's a time to share your happiness with friends and loved ones, and a time to learn and grow as you become a part of a new family. This is a time to showcase your style, whether classic or cutting edge, and a time to make choices that reflect you and your fiancé as a couple.

For me, the most beautiful, memorable brides are not the ones without flaws or flubs. Instead, I remember those women who are focused less on the quest for a day's worth of perfection and more on the deep meaning of what is unfolding before them: the promise of a lifetime's worth of love and partnership. One spring not too long ago, in the middle of a discussion about flowers and candles, one of my brides turned to me and said, "I am so lucky to be marrying this man." He wasn't even in the room. To me, that says it all.

B2B: the proposal

LINDSAY: Pampered to perfection.

Matt proposed during a surprise getaway. He had made plans for us—wine-tasting at a scenic vineyard, visiting an old lighthouse, and horseback riding on the beach. He even set up appointments for me at a local spa. When he came to pick me up from the spa, he handed me a rose and told me he had something special waiting for me back at our bed-and-breakfast. And boy, did he—our room was filled with long-stemmed roses, tons of candles, and an indoor picnic. He got down on one knee and told me how much I meant to him, and he proposed. I was so excited, I put the engagement ring on the wrong finger!

KATE: A proposal that takes the cake.

Mark proposed on the first night of our vacation in St. John. He surprised me by hiring a chef to cook and serve a special menu of Caribbean food and tropical drinks at the villa where we were staying. After dinner, the chef brought out a miniature wedding cake topped with pink flowers and accompanied by a ring box. Mark got down on one knee and asked me to marry him while waves crashed below and our favorite island music played in the background.

SARA: Tree of love.

We officially got engaged in London's Kensington Park, under a tree, on what seemed to be the only warm, sunny day that spring. We knew we wanted to get married, so it wasn't a surprise. Samir was in the UK for six weeks for work, and we'd decided that I would visit, and we'd wait until then for the official engagement. Once I arrived, it was just a matter of where to do it, so we set off that Saturday morning to the park. We walked around until we found a nice spot under a huge, old, solid tree, and he asked me to marry him. Then we both realized we were starving, so we went to celebrate with food and champagne at a local wine bar.

ELAINE: Not all rocks are created equal.

I love rocks. Jim likes to say I'm his "amateur geologist." One Sunday, we were walking along the beach and I was picking up pretty rocks and telling Jim about their history. He asked me to sit down near an old bleached-out log. As I continued to talk about the rocks in my hand, Jim took something out of his pocket. It was a ring. "Tell me about this rock," he said, and he asked me to marry him. Now I keep Jim's brilliant-cut "rock" on my finger, and the other pretty stones I picked up that day, I keep in the ring box next to my bed.

NORDIA: The ultimate stocking stuffer.

Will and I started dating just before Christmas, so a year later it was our first time really celebrating the holidays together. We'd been so busy with work that we hadn't even had time to buy ornaments for our Christmas tree, which was completely bare, except for a few strands of lights. We had plans to travel to see both of our families, but we had decided Christmas Eve would be just for us. I thought the timing made sense for him to propose, but he was so calm and casual about our plans for the day, and we'd just spent hours walking around the city, drinking hot chocolate, getting dinner, and taking in a movie. When we got home around midnight, Will suggested we open our stocking stuffers. Mine was a heart-shaped locket ornament for our tree that said OUR FIRST CHRISTMAS on the front. I opened the locket to find my favorite photo of us on one side and an engraved message on the other side. It said, WILL YOU MARRY ME? As I turned around, Will got down on one knee, and it was a very happy Christmas indeed!

simple stunning SEVEN
my best advice
before you get started

Women are like flowers—no two are the same. This is even more apparent when it comes to brides. During the process of being engaged and planning a wedding celebration, each woman develops a unique vision of who she wants to be on her wedding day, in her new married life, and beyond. Having a handle on that simple idea is the key to enjoying your process, because knowing and taking care of yourself will free you from many of the outside pressures you might encounter.

Despite what you see in the magazines or in the bridal runway show videos online, there is no perfect bride, just like there is no perfect flower. They are all perfect. Some are colorful and exuberant, while others are quietly elegant. Dramatic cherry blossoms grow on long branches, while intoxicating gardenias grow on the shortest stems. If you're a gardenia, fabulous! If you're a cherry-blossom branch, hooray! Either way, you're one lucky blossom, because you've found a partner with whom you can grow for a lifetime.

This chapter is filled with the seven pieces of advice I would give you if we were sitting down to a nice cup of coffee (or a glass of prosecco!). I would suggest that you think about all these things before you put your first deposit down on a venue or pick a date. Return to this chapter throughout your planning process and apply what works for you wherever it helps.

1. Get in touch with your own style.

This point refers not just to your fashion and beauty style, which we'll talk about later (starting on page 54). More important, it refers to *who you are as a bride*. Hint: It has a lot to do with *who you are as a person*. Consider how you like to organize things (or don't), what your decision-making process is like (quick or more considered), and what things are really important to you (your job, getting all the details of your ceremony and reception just right, enjoying lots of pampering, or all of the above plus charitable work on the weekends). There is no magic formula for getting it all done or for being the perfect engaged lady. Give yourself some time to figure out your own process and preferences, and you'll be able to tailor your own experience to suit your style.

Inspiration for your wedding details can come from any number of sources—a photograph, a fashion accessory, a time period, or even a flower. As you're thinking about mood, let yourself seek inspiration and gather notes, photos, and descriptive words to help guide you.

2. Take time to be inspired.

It's not a requirement that you should have already sketched your wedding dress and pulled fabric swatches for your tablecloths before you tell everyone you're engaged. When you're beginning your planning, don't worry about jumping into all the details. Think about the big picture first. Think about mood. Identifying the mood you want to create will help you with every single decision along the way. To find your inspiration, look everywhere—the Internet, magazines, books, your favorite stores, a neighbor's garden. Your ideas can come from anywhere, and you might build a motif or a whole color story around a single detail you find, like a flower or a stripe or a design era (Louis XIV, anyone?).

Sometimes the best wedding ideas can be found in unlikely places such as interior design books, on fashion blogs, in advertisements, even at flea markets or parks. Have fun gathering photos and notes about things you like—and even things you don't like. I always find having these visuals very helpful, and even when I meet with brides who have pulled different looks or seem to like opposing colors, I can usually spot a link between them. Visual cues and descriptive words will help you identify and communicate the unique mood you want to create for your one-of-a-kind wedding.

You may find that family and friends are asking you a lot of questions about what you're planning. "What are your colors?" "Did you get your dress yet?" "What are the bridesmaids wearing?" Don't let these queries fluster you, especially in the beginning, when design

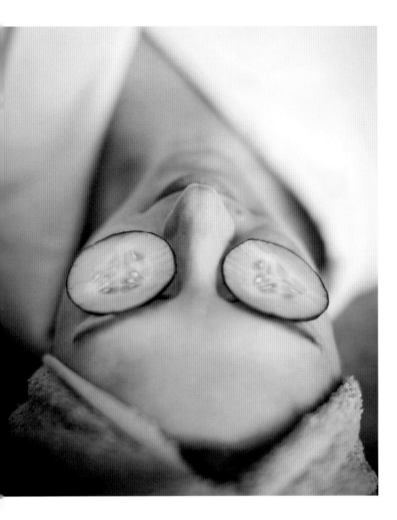

Did you know? Self-pampering is a job requirement for every bride. It can take whatever form you like—a massage or facial at a fancy spa, or just a long, hot bubble bath at home. The important thing is to take time to take care of you.

details may not yet be clear. Deflect Nosy Nanettes with a simple stunning response: "I'm just over the moon with excitement, but we want everything to be a surprise, so you'll have to wait and see!"

3. Don't try this alone.

They don't give awards at the wedding for heroic bridal behavior. Brides often feel responsible for making sure everyone is happy. They see all the smiling brides in magazines and think they're supposed to make the process look effortless. But the fact is, a wedding is all about people coming together to celebrate a special moment, to embrace a couple as part of the family and the community. So why not ask for help when you need it? Why not involve your friends and family (and of course your fiancé!) with fun projects to personalize the wedding, and to help out with errands and tasks when you're feeling overwhelmed?

A good friend of mine (and bride-to-be) recently asked a group of friends to come over and help with prepping her wedding invitations and addressing envelopes to her four hundred guests. She saved tons of money on calligraphy with our help (even after the cost of pizza and prosecco), and our whole group had a blast, laughing and talking while we worked. This personal project brought us all even closer, as we pulled together in honor of the happy couple, and when our invitations came in the mail, we all had happy memories of a wonderful shared experience.

4. **Remember, your wedding lasts for a day (okay, maybe a weekend). Your marriage is forever.**

Sometimes the pressure of putting on a perfect party can take the focus off what's really important. Although you'll certainly have to give your attention to all the little details, like choosing a menu and deciding who'll make the toasts at your reception, make sure to keep it all in perspective. This attitude really comes in handy when things get stressful—after all, what's most important is not the perfect shade of coral for your peonies, or the linen napkin versus the cotton one, or the caviar station that throws your budget out of whack—it's the love and bond you share with friends, family, and your future husband.

5. **Slow down and enjoy your engagement.**

This can be hard to hear, especially for busy women who are juggling a lot even in a normal week. While planning your wedding, there might be a time (or 12) when you feel like pulling your hair (or someone else's) out. But even when things are going swimmingly (which hopefully will be most of the time), treat this phase of your life as extra-special. Think of it as not just "wedding-planning time" or "gotta-get-stuff-done time," but as a time to celebrate in and of itself. After all, you don't want to end up on your wedding day feeling like the whole thing just passed you by while you were busy with tasks and to-dos. Of course, if you do find you need to pull out some hair, make sure it's someone else's, or at least leave enough on your own head to clip in your extensions.

6. **Take the opportunity to pamper yourself.**

Indulge in things you really love, whether it's a yoga class, a deep-tissue massage, a funny old movie, a glass of champagne, or a run in the park. Light a scented candle and take a warm bubble bath. Cook a delicious, healthy meal. Daydream about happiness and your honeymoon and the amazing adventures you're about to have. Talk to someone who always makes you laugh. Get plenty of sleep whenever you can. Go for manicures, or invite friends over and do each other's nails. Curl up on a comfy couch and browse through your favorite books and magazines.

7. **Love out loud.**

Tell your man how much you love him. Tell him why you love him. Shower him with affection. Hold his hand. Sit on his lap. Notice the little things he does. Praise him when he kisses you just the way you like it. Praise him when he helps you pick out invitations (I don't care what you say, most guys just don't really care about fonts). Text him sexy notes. Smile at him. Set a tone of sweetness that will last far beyond the wedding.

Note: Out-loud loving applies to friends and family as well, except for the kisses. And sexy text messages.

what's a BRIDE TO DO?

traditions, roles, and responsibilities

Center of attention. Ringleader. Researcher. Diplomat. Design maven. Hostess extraordinaire. Fashionista. Honoree. Taskmaster. Juggler. Loving daughter. Good friend. Team captain. Dancing queen. Sexy, sweet partner. Party planner. Etiquette expert. Foodie. Accountant. Gracious recipient of gifts. Knowing negotiator. Master multitasker.

Sound like anyone you know? Being a bride requires, among many other things, a chameleon-like ability to switch hats quickly and often. Use this chapter as your cheat sheet to make the process easier and, frankly, way more fun.

what do they want from you?

Traditionally, the bride was responsible for planning the entire wedding (with the exception of the rehearsal dinner, which was the groom's parents' territory), along with her family. "Family" originally meant "mom" for all intents and purposes (or sometimes grandmothers and aunts, too). These days, there can be any combination of people involved in the process of planning, from just the couple themselves to the whole family (or even both families). But even with this more modern configuration, you, as the bride, are really the team leader, and it's your responsibility (and your right!) to guide the process.

Here's a list of some key bridal responsibilities to consider, along with a basic description of each and some solid advice to get you started. I've pared it down (and it still seems like quite a list, doesn't it?) to the essentials, and you'll discover your own sub-topics as you get into your own planning process. Of course, your groom and family can and should be as involved as you like, and you can and should certainly delegate some of these elements, or parts of them, according to what works best for you.

When you do delegate a role or responsibility, just make sure to provide any guidelines or priorities up front, and then really try to give the person you've asked for help the time and space to take care of the task.

Creating and managing a budget.

Back in the day, budgeting was much more of a parental role, and wedding celebrations were often much simpler, requiring just a few flowers and some cake and champagne at the reception. You'll need to determine who's paying for the wedding (you, your parents, or both sets of parents, for example), and I suggest you hold frank, open discussions about money right up front to save you time, trouble, and conflict later.

Throughout the process, someone will need to keep track of deposits paid, payments due, and overall budget numbers, to make sure you're on point. Decide in advance who this budget point person will be. In my office, we use Excel to track budgets, and it works really well, as you can project what you want to spend, then plug in the actuals as you make choices and secure services.

Choosing a venue.

I always say that choosing where to celebrate is probably the most important decision you make about your wedding. Again, traditionally the bride's family would host the wedding, and parents would often have a large role in determining where to celebrate (banquet hall, backyard, or church or temple fellowship room, for example). Now, I can't imagine a couple letting anyone else choose their venue, although parents are often involved in the process.

Much like budgeting, when searching for the right place to celebrate, keep my advice from the previous chapter in mind. What mood do you hope to create for

your wedding? If you want an elegant, traditional black-tie affair, start with clubs, museums, and historic spaces. If you envision a more whimsical, bohemian mood, look for funky lofts, a winery, or an art gallery. If symbolism is important to you, look to where you come from or a place that is special to you both as a couple. If you love to travel, pick the most glorious spot you can imagine!

The responsibility of choosing a venue really needs to be shared by you and your fiancé, as well as anyone else who might be a decision maker or a financial contributor to the celebration. But you should determine in advance who will start the research and how you'll set parameters, such as distance from your home, number of guests you need to accommodate, and costs.

You should also determine what the roles will be as far as first visits (perhaps his job is more flexible than yours, or perhaps you both have a weekend off soon) and who you'll include in the negotiation process once you've narrowed down your selections and requested a contract.

Also keep in mind whether you'll be married at the same site as your reception. If you belong to a house of worship, you'll want to understand their wedding requirements and timing before finding your reception venue. If you plan to be married at your reception site, make sure that is permissible and practical, and inquire about additional fees for this service.

What kind of wedding do you imagine? Whether it's a luncheon in a lush vineyard, a cosmopolitan celebration in the big city, or a breezy beach bash, where you choose to celebrate will influence every other decision you make.

Hiring key service providers.

Once you've booked your venue and set your date, you can start assembling your team. I suggest beginning with a caterer (if one is not already a part of your venue package) and a stationer or invitation designer. Save-the-date cards and invitations can take a while to produce, so getting started early is a good idea if you have the time.

If you need to find an officiant, I suggest addressing this right away—especially if you're planning an interfaith or untraditional ceremony. Next, choose your music providers and photographer (these folks always book up first), videographer (if it's not a part of your photography package), hair and makeup artists, and, finally, transportation.

As you're hiring your team, keep in mind that it should be someone's responsibility to get every detail in writing. You should have a signed document from every service provider, and you should keep them organized in a file or binder for easy reference. Chances are you'll need to check the contract at least once before the big day.

Planning group accommodations and transportation for your guests.

It's considered gracious for the bride and groom to pre-book blocks of rooms or at least to suggest good hotels in the area close to the wedding. Think about how many of your guests might need a place to stay, and call local hotels, a travel agent, or your chamber of commerce for help. This is one area of responsibility that could easily be shared or taken on by your groom or another family member. Just make sure the hotel doesn't require you to financially guarantee the rooms you're blocking, and get all the details regarding cutoff dates for special rates.

Planning the ceremony.

The bride and groom must share this responsibility with their officiant or religious leader. Depending on your situation and preferences, you may have more or less input into the specifics of your service, and you may involve parents in this process. Discuss any concerns with your fiancé and then meet with your officiant(s) to review details. If you'll print a program, I also suggest sending a copy for your officiant(s) to review before you go to press.

Selecting and communicating with your bridal party.

Traditionally, the bride and groom each choose their attendants, and for many years it was the norm to have equal numbers of bridesmaids and groomsmen. These days, there are no restrictions, and you are welcome to choose whomever you like to support you throughout the process and to stand up with you on the big day.

As a bride, you not only have to choose your wedding party, but what they wear, and even what flowers they'll carry. Let your choices reflect your style and the feeling you want to create.

Once you've chosen your bridal party, I suggest you have a conversation with your "honor" attendants (best man, maid of honor, matron of honor, etc.) to discuss how best they can help you, their roles in the celebration, and how you'll communicate about wedding-related issues.

I also suggest sending regular e-mail updates to your wedding party (once a month or so) to keep them up-to-date in an organized manner. They'll appreciate this much more than random e-mails every few days.

Communicating with your guests.

This is probably one of the roles that surprises brides and grooms most often. I think they don't realize how many people are going to contact them with congratulations, questions, concerns, issues, and just about anything else you can think of. Brides skilled in diplomacy will have no problems at all, but others may find themselves overwhelmed. I suggest starting a wedding website (there are lots of services online to help you) to provide basic info and also creating a wedding e-mail address, such as jordanandjohnswedding@gmail.com. You can provide a list of FAQs on the wedding website to answer any common concerns. And with your wedding e-mail address, you'll avoid getting wedding

As a bride, you'll likely find yourself thinking about all kinds of small details—napkin folds, menu cards, even chair accents. Let your creativity shine!

messages and questions all day at work. When you have a few minutes to answer questions or write to family and friends, you can switch into that role and do what you need to do.

Making decisions about food, flowers, music, invitations, and other details.

This is a role some brides love and some fear. Brides tell me that the thing that surprises them the most is how many decisions there are to make. This plate or that plate? Salmon or bass? Sauvignon blanc or chardonnay? This song or that one? My best advice is that you should try to decide in advance which will be your main areas of responsibility and which you'll leave to your fiancé. Of course, if you prefer to be co-captains on everything, that's great, too, but you should discuss the process early on, because there will be a lot of choosing to do, a lot of e-mails and phone calls, and some meetings. How will you each participate? There's more good advice on this topic in the Communication 101 chapter (page 44).

Selecting and coordinating your gown, outfits, and accessories for all wedding-related events.

This is the fun stuff. I will tell you that bridal dresses can take a while to order, so if you have time, start early. If you don't, don't fret about fashion—read the chapters on all these topics starting on page 54.

Approving or suggesting wedding-party attire.

You'll be responsible for guiding your attendants toward what you want them to wear, and you should take into account the season, their body types, and their budgets. As for your groom's attendants, speak with your fiancé to determine what the process should be. If he's fashion-oriented (or even if he's not!), he might have strong opinions about how he sees himself and his attendants being dressed for the big day.

In addition, you'll need to communicate with your parents about what they're wearing. Tradition says that the bride's mother gets to decide her color and style before the groom's mother, but these days, it's really up to each couple and their families to determine what works best. My advice: Let them wear whatever they like! Remember when I told you in the Introduction that I'd help you dispense with what just doesn't matter? What matters is that your moms and dads wear something they like and feel comfortable in. Trust me on this one.

Attending wedding-related parties, such as engagement parties, showers, and the rehearsal dinner.

Your role here, aside from being the guest of honor, is to be gracious and thankful. Also, make sure you let folks know of any major scheduling conflicts in advance (final exams at school, a big business trip, etc.).

You're expected to provide information about your registry or other concerns your host might have, to be on time and charming, and to offer a gift and personal note to anyone who hosts a party for you. You are obligated to write a personal thank-you note to anyone who gives you a gift.

Just one essential piece of toasting etiquette advice here—and you can apply this to all your wedding related events. Did you know that when folks toast to you, you're not supposed to raise your glass?

Securing a marriage license and attending to other legal matters.

You must research your local regulations for obtaining a marriage license and follow procedures to make sure you have everything in order before the wedding. You can ask your groom to do the research, but chances are you'll have to appear together in person to apply for the license to wed.

If applicable, you'll want to have details about any prenuptial agreements ironed out well in advance of the celebration.

If you'd like to change your name after marriage, I suggest waiting until after you return from your honeymoon, as you can't legally make the change without your marriage certificate, and you don't want to have travel documents that don't match.

Choosing bridesmaids' dresses that will please and flatter everyone can seem like a daunting task. Remember, they don't necessarily need to match, but they should coordinate with one another.

Giving thoughtful gifts to your attendants.
Their role is to support you. Your role is to appreciate them. Heartfelt notes of acknowledgment, toasts to their fabulousness, a luncheon in their honor, and quality gifts are all part of your responsibility.

# of course, you might add to the above:

Keeping everyone happy (or at least on speaking terms).

Navigating merging families and parental personalities—not to mention bridesmaid issues and annoying siblings—are all the responsibility of you and your husband-to-be.

The best thing you can do for yourself to minimize your own stress is to understand that most of the time when conflict arises, it's not about you. It's not about your wedding. It's just that weddings bring out things in people that might normally be hidden. My

If ever you find yourself frustrated with friends, family, or even your fiancé, take a moment to close your eyes and imagine yourself on the big day, wearing your new ring and toasting your loved ones with a glass of bubbly. I guarantee you this technique will help you keep the small stuff in perspective.

advice: Be gracious and diplomatic when you can. Be polite and firm when you can't.

Answering questions, even if they're silly.

"What does 'festive attire' really mean?" "Can I bring my pet ferret?" "Can I bring the guy I just started going out with?" Yes, it is your responsibility to see that these questions get answered, unless you're prepared to deal with what might happen if you just ignore them (pet ferrets on the dance floor?). As I've suggested, create a wedding e-mail address and answer these questions when you have time and a chance to consider your response.

Putting out fires.

Your fiancé is arguing with the band. Your mom cannot get your future mother-in-law to return her calls. The shop making your bridesmaids' dresses went out of business. While you'll likely have to deal with one or two (hopefully minor) crises during your wedding-planning process, understand that you can't solve everything. When you really need to get involved, take it one step at a time. Get all the information first, then consider your options, then make a decision about how to solve the issue. As always, ask for help when you need it.

Picking up the slack.

Think of this part of your bridal experience as excellent preparation for motherhood. Sometimes people just aren't as motivated or efficient or brilliant or organized or prepared as you are, so you'll want to jump in to help get stuff done or to keep things moving according to your own sense of timing. But before you do, take a hard look at whether you really need to move now, or whether you could give that person or situation a little more time to resolve itself without stressing you out. If you do need to step in, put on your Polite Team Leader hat and try to be motivational without being confrontational.

Laying down the law, but only when absolutely necessary.

If a really difficult situation comes up and you must "flip the switch" (my term for moving into "oh, no you didn't" mode), take a deep breath first. Whether it's a serious conflict with a vendor or a personal issue with a family member, if possible, I suggest you sleep on it and approach the problem with a refreshed mind and a clear head. If something is really troubling, follow my advice and be polite but firm in your response to the situation. It is your wedding, and ultimately, you should be the arbiter of what is or isn't acceptable.

two more bridal roles, do they apply to you?

1. SOCIALLY RESPONSIBLE HOSTESS.

Weddings are wonderful, bountiful occasions. Many times, large numbers of people are involved, and

because of the fleeting nature of the celebration itself, an incredible amount of waste can be an unhappy by-product of the happiest day of your life. If you like, give some thought to how you can minimize waste and maximize the joy of sharing your happiness with others in positive ways. Here are a few ideas:

- **Choose environmentally friendly materials wherever they make sense.** More and more stationers, for example, are offering designs on recycled paper, printed with soy-based inks. Soy candles are becoming easier to find. Every little bit makes a difference, especially when you consider there are about 2.5 million weddings in the U.S. every year.

- **Use what you have.** Is there anything in your world you could recycle into a fabulous wedding accent? Some old floral vases you have sitting around in the garage? A chandelier in Aunt Joan's basement? A basket in your kitchen that you could decorate to hold your flower girl's petals? You'll save money and you can feel good about reusing things rather than buying new stuff.

- **Buy local.** Ask your caterer to use local ingredients on your menu. Choose flowers that are in season and grown in your area. These choices not only benefit your community by supporting local businesses, they also lower the impact you create from shipping and transporting items over a long distance.

- **Make your guest favors count.** Plant a tree on behalf of each guest who attends your wedding, or give them all miniature saplings to plant in memory of your happy day (see Resource Guide for where to buy them).

- **Register to help your favorite cause** instead of or in addition to other gift registries that you may set up. The Internet offers many options for setting up a registry to benefit a wide variety of charitable organizations.

- **Donate leftover items wherever possible.** Find a local school or arts organization that would love to receive your extra vases, candles, glitter, ribbon, etc. At my company, we have been thrilled to find partners in our community who make great use of our leftovers. I often get sweet letters from the grateful recipients, and that always makes my day! If you want to donate food or flowers, you'll have to check into that closely, as regulations may come into play. For example, some hospitals will not accept unsolicited floral arrangements, and some food pantries restrict what types of items can be accepted.

What's in a name?

The term "groom" evolved from an ancient word meaning "male child." The term "bride" comes from an ancient word for "cook." Kinda makes you think, right?

B2B: what surprised you about planning your wedding?

DEBBY: All the fun details.

I was surprised by how much fun it was! I really loved thinking about the flowers and the invitations and favors and trying to bring personalized touches to all parts of the day. It was stressful at times, but overall I had a fantastic time planning it and found the process to be very romantic.

INGRID: Timing is everything.

I couldn't believe how far in advance certain popular vendors, such as photographers, get locked in. The sooner you book key people and services, the more flexibility you have to get what you want.

ERICA: Decisions, decisions.

The number of details was overwhelming. I knew I had to find a location, a band, flowers, and a dress. But lighting and sound—those weren't even on my radar. The number of contracts we needed to review and sign was surprising to me as well. At times it was easy to forget we were planning a wedding. It felt more like a gala event!

2. ONCE AND FUTURE BRIDE.

If you're planning a wedding other than your first, you may have questions about what is appropriate in terms of everything—your dress, the size of your party, whether you can have bridesmaids, whom you should invite. In the past, folks might've expected a second wedding (or a third) to be smaller and more low-key than the first one, but that's just not the case anymore.

The bottom line is you should have the party you wish to have, and it should be a personal celebration of your love. If you are low-key folks, then let the event be mellow. If you've "been there, done that" with the big wedding, then keep it smaller and more intimate.

If, however, they didn't have strapless gowns the first time you went down the aisle, and you really want to invite a couple hundred of your closest friends, my advice would take the form of a question: Why not? Of course you'll do it all in good taste and with simple stunning style, so you've got nothing to worry about. Your role is, like all brides, to be considerate of others but true to yourself. Have fun with it!

the organized BRIDE
strategies for staying sane

Wouldn't it be wonderful if we could just take a vacation from our regular responsibilities while we're busy planning one of the most important days of our lives? If only there was a "bridal leave" policy in effect to allow us a stress-free window of time to get it all together? "Dear Mr. President . . ."

Everyone always talks about wedding planning as if it's the same process for everyone, and as if every bride has the same timeline and the same priorities. From having worked with so many brides, I know this isn't true. This is your wedding, and it and you are one-of-a-kind. I believe you can make the whole process more efficient and more fun if you spend a little time thinking about who you are and what really works best for you.

This chapter is filled with ideas and advice to help you understand your own needs, organize your planning process, manage your time, and navigate the delicate balance between wedding work, work-work, and your life.

make a plan for planning

Think about the following five questions before you jump headlong into visiting venues, choosing caterers, and researching bands. They'll help you keep your head on straight and keep the process moving along smoothly while you simultaneously have a life.

QUESTION 1:

What's your organizational style?

In general, would you describe yourself as organizationally challenged or do you thrive on keeping track of lots of details? If the former is true, you might consider hiring a planner or asking a very organized friend to help you stay on track. If you're great with details and research, you might be just fine on your own, although I still recommend hiring or appointing someone to deal with last-minute issues on the wedding day (or weekend).

QUESTION 2:

Is your work schedule nutso?

Will you be scheduling appointments around a busy workweek? If so, use a calendar or an online planning tool to block out available times for meetings and general wedding-planning duties—and stick to it. Tell prospective vendors about your schedule limitations up front and make sure they'll accommodate special meeting times.

QUESTION 3:

Are you on the road a lot?

Will you be traveling frequently during your engagement? If you will be away from home often, ask your service providers to streamline meetings and set up conference calls instead of having in-person meetings whenever possible. There are many free or low-cost teleconference and web-meeting services available. You can sign up for them online and ask everyone (vendors, your fiancé, your parents, etc.) to dial and/or log in at the appointed time, even if you're not in town.

QUESTION 4:

How do you choose?

Are you someone who makes decisions quickly and easily, or do you prefer more time to consider a variety of options and do detailed research? If you are the kind of person who has difficulty picking out a restaurant for dinner, it's a good idea to have one other trusted friend or family member involved in important meetings so you can share concerns and get their opinions on the spot. It's best if the same family member or two can be with you throughout the process, as having too many opinions can add to indecision—you know, too many cooks . . .

QUESTION 5:

Do you know what you want?

Do you have a pretty clear vision of your celebration, or could you use some guidance? If you really don't yet know what you want, I suggest hiring an event planner, who can help you distill your ideas and bring them to life. A good planner is an acute listener who can take your inspirations and guide you through the process of turning them into memorable event details.

Once you've explored the answers to these questions, you can think about how best to structure your tasks and allot your time. If, for example, you are a busy professional and you travel often for work, you might want to consider hiring a wedding planner to help you throughout the process by coordinating your meetings, evaluating vendors, and managing the team, so you can direct without getting mired down in all the small stuff.

get in the driver's seat

Ask yourself the questions below to make sure you have a handle on who is running the show and determining what the goals really are.

QUESTION 1:

Who's in charge?

I once was blindsided by a very, shall we say, "proactive" mother-of-the-bride who told me at our first (brideless) meeting that she and her daughter had discussed everything and had made decisions about the wedding in advance. Apparently this busy young woman, who was finishing college, couldn't make time to get away from school. One day, when we were about to send the absentee bride's save-the-date cards to the printer (approved by the M.O.B., of course), my cell phone rang. A sweet voice asked me, "Karen, is my mother planning my wedding without me?"

The point of this story is that, unlike *this* bride, you should make sure you determine who, aside from you and your fiancé, will have input on important decisions about your wedding. Will you have help from your mother, his mother, a trusted friend, a sister, or all of the above? Or none of the above?

Of course, you'll have to take into account who has actually offered to pitch in, who is located near enough to you to be involved in meetings, and other factors (such as who you *want* to be involved!), but if you can establish early on who the key decision makers will be, you can take charge and streamline the process by inviting those folks to big meetings, copying them on e-mails, and keeping them in the loop.

QUESTION 2:

What's his deal?

Remember: He's engaged, too. But do you really know how involved your fiancé will want to be leading up to the wedding celebration? Does he want to attend every meeting, or does he envision you doing more of the legwork, and then bringing him in for final approval on things like music, catering, and photography?

I've seen many couples struggle as they discover that their priorities or their ideas about the division of labor might not be the same. An open discussion of how you each prefer to work on this complicated project can be very helpful.

Sharing your needs and feelings—and listening to his—will guide you toward a greater sense of sharing in both the responsibilities and the joy of planning this special event.

QUESTION 3:

What are your couple priorities?

Sit with your fiancé. Each of you should make a list of the three most important elements of your wedding. Is it the time of year? The size of the party? The budget? The music? Food? For each couple, it's different. Once you have your lists, discuss and combine them to come up with your couple priority list—you can have up to five priorities combined. Let these priorities be your signposts, helping to guide you when you have choices to make or budget to allot.

QUESTION 4:

What will help you help yourself?

Do what you need to do *for yourself* to make the process fun and enjoyable. There is a lot of unanticipated stress that comes with planning something as important as a wedding. Your job may suddenly change and become more time-consuming. You may find that unexpected opinions and advice are popping up randomly from friends and family. You may not know how to handle sticky situations that arise.

You can help yourself by setting up your process in a way that has the best chance of working for you—whether that means limiting wedding appointments mainly to evenings and weekends, holding once-a-week wedding conference calls with your parents, or allotting an hour a day at lunchtime to deal with vendors and details. Create a solid structure and you'll set yourself up for more success and less stress.

organize the big two: time and stuff

Let's talk time. If I just say "organize your time," I'm sure that you'll roll your eyes at me. The fact is, there is no "bridal leave" policy, and there likely never will be. I often get e-mails from brides at midnight or later, because that's when they're finally able to sit down and read a contract or look at an invitation proof. As a planner, I often schedule meetings during a client's lunch hour or in the early morning so that her work won't be

Who knew? Take the time to discuss your couple priorities early in the process. How do each of you rate the importance of elements such as music, food, wine, and décor? An open discussion will help you focus your time and energy toward a result that will please you both.

Did you know?

The average length of an engagement in the United States is about 16 months.

impacted. In fact, recently I met a bride and her mom at the flower market at 7:30 A.M.! It can be done.

Of course, you know your own schedule best, so my first piece of advice would be to make a personal planning calendar to help guide your process. Take a look at the big picture first, and divide the time between now and the wedding into three phases. Once you have the three phases mapped out, you can use an online planning calendar, buy a notebook planner, or make your own. Here are some essential components to the three phases.

Phase 1: The big picture and key people

In the first phase, you'll want to address and complete all the big tasks—securing a date and venue, hiring your team, choosing your wedding party, buying a dress, and planning your invitations. This way, you'll get your infrastructure in place, and you'll avoid any rush fees.

Phase 2: Design and details

During the middle phase, you'll examine all the core details. You'll start your design discussions with your floral designer, make sure your bridesmaids have dresses,

buy your rings, and plan the honeymoon. You should start thinking about your ceremony and where you might want to have the rehearsal dinner and/or a post-wedding brunch. You'll decide where you want to stay on your wedding night and make sure your wedding website is up and running.

Phase 3: Almost there

In the home stretch, you'll hold calls or meetings with each of your vendors to discuss final arrangements and timing for things like formal portraits, song selections for the ceremony and reception, final flower selections, and menu choices. I also suggest hosting a final walk-through with key folks (your venue representative, caterer, band leader, and florist) to make sure that all who need to be in touch with each other are, and that everyone is on the same page. If you don't have a professional planner, you'll also want to appoint someone, other than yourself or a member of your bridal party, to be the point person for vendors on the big day. Of course your venue management team will help keep things on track, but it's a great idea to have someone close to you who can speak with vendors on the big day if anything comes up. That person should be at your final walk-through, shaking hands and making friends.

HAVE A STRATEGY SESSION

Once you have your planning schedule set up, I recommend you invite anyone who will have a key decision-making role to join you for a "strategy session" to discuss the planning process. I do this for every single one of my clients. It's usually the bride and groom, sometimes a mom or two, and occasionally a dad thrown in for good measure.

We sit down and talk through how each person in the room feels about each major element of the wedding, such as food, music, photography, videography (this one always starts a good debate), invitations, and overall room design. This open, preliminary meeting is great because everyone gets a chance to express their opinions and any concerns they might have *before* anyone is hired or any major commitments are made. You might be surprised at what you find out at this meeting, but it's better to know now than later in the process.

FIVE GOOD REASONS TO HIRE A WEDDING PLANNER

1. You travel a lot or are extremely busy at work and unable to spend time setting up meetings and dealing with wedding minutiae. A planner can help maximize your time by taking care of some or all of the behind-the-scenes work, like returning phone calls and requesting proposals from vendors.

2. You don't have a lot of help. If trusted members of your immediate family are unavailable, your best friend lives far away, and your fiancé says things like, "Whatever you want, babe" when asked about details, you might benefit from having someone with whom you can trade ideas and discuss details and options.

3. You're not sure what you want. If you feel like you're floundering and flip-flopping, and you can't decide whether you want a backyard wedding or a country club soirée, a planner can help you understand the pros and cons of each, and can keep you on track throughout the process, so that your decisions are in line with your priorities and maintain your overall vision.

4. You're not so great with details and organization. If the idea of keeping track of contracts and payment schedules and timelines and regulations and blocks of hotel rooms and all the other little things gives you a rash, it might be time to call in a pro. She can deal with the administrative stuff, leaving you free to be the big-picture bride.

5. You want to maximize your wedding budget. This may sound counterintuitive, because hiring a planner certainly comes with a cost. But a good planner can project what a reasonable budget is for your celebration, advise you where to spend and where to save, and leverage their own relationships with vendors to get you better deals.

GOT BINDER?

Now, let's talk stuff. Weddings generate lots of stuff, not the least of which is paper: brochures, contracts, business cards, lists, color swatches, paper samples, sketches, and invoices, to name just a few. So whether you buy a wedding-planning binder or make your own at home, you should create a special place to store your notes, inspirations, contracts, and other key information. You can use a simple notebook with pockets, an accordion file, or a wedding-planning binder like my *Simple Stunning Wedding Organizer* (see Resource Guide for more information).

I also recommend creating a file on your computer for digital copies of all your wedding research

B2B: what was your planning process like?

LINDSAY: Get help.
A wedding planner really helped us. In order for the night to flow effortlessly, there are so many little things that need to be managed. These things make such a big difference when it comes to your guests' enjoyment. A pro comes in handy because she already knows what all of the potential pitfalls are and can help you avoid them.

SARA: Make it happen. Sooner.
In retrospect, I would have shortened my planning process. We hadn't been together for a very long time when we got engaged, so a more drawn-out engagement seemed prudent. It surprised me, but waiting more than a year ended up feeling like forever. If I were to do it over, I'd plan a less lengthy engagement—enough time to enjoy the process, but not enough time to worry and second-guess every decision.

DEBBY: Pay for quality.
Ever heard the saying "Pay peanuts, get monkeys"? Well, everything I tried to do on the cheap ended up looking cheap, and I found myself regretting the decisions. In contrast, the places where I invested money to get quality services or goods always paid off.

ELAINE: Stay organized and in control.
Buy a wedding organizer, keep detailed records, and retain every receipt. Also, write thank-you notes as you receive gifts. I can't imagine what would have happened if I had waited until after the wedding to write them all.

and documents. This way, you have them easily at hand throughout your process. And of course you'll want to back up your hard drive often.

balancing work-work with wedding work

This is definitely one of the top issues brides deal with every day. Are you struggling with it, too? After all, there are phone calls that need to be made during business hours, and some vendors don't make after-hours appointments. And of course there's always a ton of research that needs to be done on the Internet: blogs, wedding websites, bridal runway-fashion videos—they're so tempting, and before you know it, there goes an hour (or four).

If you're self-employed, it can be easier to schedule wedding time as needed, but you might also find yourself spending more hours than you should surfing the Web for bridesmaids' dress options while you should be out courting new clients.

If you work for others, there is the ethical dilemma—how much time can you spend attending to wedding-related tasks while you're on the clock? The answer varies of course, according to your responsibilities and the demands of your workplace. If you're a neurosurgeon, chances are . . . well, you get the picture.

A good solution: When you find yourself in need of workday time to deal with wedding issues, make plans to take care of things on your lunch hour. If you have access to the Internet, let your boss and coworkers know of your plan, in case they see you eating lunch at your desk, reading invitation proofs. You could also ask your boss if you could come in a half hour early and take an hour and a half for lunch to allow ample time for meetings.

If you have to run out to an appointment, ask if your photographer or band leader can meet you near your office—you'd be surprised how accommodating some vendors will be. They deal with busy brides all the time. In general, as long as you manage your workday wedding time-outs carefully, you are not likely to have a problem.

WEDDING CHATTER

Resist the temptation (and it is tempting) to talk about your wedding nonstop at work. Although your coworkers will undoubtedly be happy for you, realize that your wedding is not their priority. And if you work in a cubicle or open area where your conversations can be overheard, take special care to be discreet. If you need to have a long (or heated) call about anything, try to have these conversations outside your workplace.

I also suggest starting a free e-mail account (think Hotmail, Gmail, Yahoo, etc.) that's used just for wedding communications. This way, wedding-related e-mails aren't flooding in and distracting you all day, and when you take time to check this account, you'll have all your correspondence in one place. Plus, after the wedding, you won't be bothered with e-mail newsletters from wedding vendors.

communication 101

keeping lines clear with everyone involved

A wedding is a complicated event, filled with merging families, incredible emotions, tons of details, and—sometimes—opportunities for misunderstanding. There are so many people to talk to and so many things to talk about: food, drinks, timing, ceremonies, relationships, etiquette issues, money—you name it—it's all there!

Taking some time to think about communication with everyone involved in your wedding (and your life!) is not such a bad idea, and it can help you streamline the process and keep the lines of communication open and operational.

This chapter is designed to help you explore your communication style. You'll also find suggestions for how to structure some of the dialogues you'll likely need to have with vendors and others along the way.

line 1: you and your fiancé

Planning your wedding might be the first big project you and your fiancé have ever had to tackle as a team. Communicating openly with each other is one way to ensure a smoother planning process (and a happier relationship overall).

One of the first things to consider is your general personal style when it comes to communicating. Are you chatty? Do you like to share details and get multiple opinions before making a decision, or do you tend to work solo, keeping your thoughts and feelings under wraps? Do you think with your heart? Are you quick with an answer or do you prefer a considered response?

Once you've thought about your own style of communication, think next about your fiancé. How are you similar? When you disagree on something, how do each of you respond?

COUPLES COMMUNICATION QUIZ

If you like, try this exercise with your fiancé. Write the following questions on two sheets of paper, then fill them out separately and review your answers together.

1. Five words I would use to describe my communication style are

_____

_____

2. Choose the answer(s) that describe(s) you best: When I'm making a decision, I

☐ am quick to decide and don't look back.

☐ often second-guess myself.

☐ need all the info and time to sleep on it.

☐ like to shop around.

☐ would rather have someone else decide.

☐ like to come in late in the process when the options have already been narrowed down.

3. When I'm excited about something, I usually

_____

_____

4. When someone disagrees with me, I typically

_____

_____

5. If we should disagree about something related to the wedding, it would help me if you would

_____

_____

6. When it comes to the wedding, I'm most excited about

_____

_____

and I'm most concerned about

_____

7. Three things I love about you are

a) _____

b) _____

c) _____

These insights may help start an interesting discussion about priorities and how you want to keep the lines of communication open throughout the complex process of planning your wedding. You may learn that he's more concerned about his parents than you thought, or that it would help him if you'd narrow down choices before asking his opinion. If you each take what you learn to heart and apply it to your discussions, you'll be less likely to get frustrated with each other or disappoint each other.

And if the discussions don't go well, focus on the answers to question seven.

line 2: family and friends

You'll need to communicate different things to different people throughout the process of planning your celebration. Make a promise to keep key players informed and on the same page. Here are some ideas:

YOUR PARENTS

Depending on how involved both sets of parents will be, you can determine a process for communicating with them. At the beginning, discuss your preferred mode of

hint

YOUR PRIORITIES ARE NOT ALWAYS THEIR PRIORITIES.

What I mean is, while bridesmaids, friends, and close family members all care deeply about your celebration, they don't care as much as you do. And that's okay. Understand that your attendants or your parents might be working on a slightly different timeline (or energy level) than you, so try to avoid being a taskmaster if at all possible, and give folks a chance to do things at their own pace.

contact with them. You might choose to host a monthly planning meeting to review progress and update to-do lists, or if your folks are farther away, schedule regular conference calls. Of course, if you talk to your mom every day, this might not be necessary, but it still can be a good idea to have recap meetings on a regular basis to keep everyone in the loop.

OTHER FAMILY

Weddings can bring out issues with siblings, stepparents, children from previous marriages, and other relatives, depending on your family dynamics. Some relatives may expect to play a certain role in your celebration, or they may have preconceived ideas about elements you hadn't even thought about. You probably

have some idea where difficulties might arise, and I encourage you to think about those scenarios so that you can be prepared to deal with things that might come up.

Always be sure to listen wholeheartedly to any family concerns, and to take others' feelings into account when making major decisions that might affect the family. If you choose not to follow the advice or direction given by someone close to you, be gracious, express your appreciation of their thoughts and ideas, and make sure that they know that they have been heard. Of course, ultimately, you must be true to your own wishes.

Did you know?

It's not appropriate to communicate gift registry information on your wedding invitations. The details of where you're registered are supposed to be communicated by word of mouth. Of course, it has become acceptable to post links to your registry on a wedding website if you're so inclined, and guests do find it convenient.

BRIDAL PARTY

When it's important, keep communication personal. For example, when asking people to be in your bridal party, a mass e-mail just won't suffice. If your key people are far away, or if your schedules won't allow for face-to-face meetings, making phone calls is perfectly fine.

When it comes to details of events or timing, however, e-mails can be a great way to communicate with the group. I do recommend writing a heartfelt card or letter to each member of your bridal party, along with any folks who will offer readings or participate in your ceremony or reception in other special ways, to convey your thanks and to let them know how much their support means to you.

GUESTS

If you'd like to send a save-the-date card, feel free to get creative. A postcard or note is fine, and some eco-friendly couples are opting to use e-mail for this kind of communication. As I mentioned in the Organized Bride chapter, a wedding website is another great way to save paper and share important information (along with stories and photos). Although I am eco-friendly myself, I still believe that a wedding invitation (as well as a thank-you card) merits a real piece of paper. That being said, I certainly encourage the use of environmentally responsible materials in the printing process, such as recycled or treeless papers, and soy-based inks.

Your bridal party is filled with folks who love and support you. Make sure to keep lines of communication open with them throughout the process, address any concerns they might have, and thank them for being a part of your celebration.

As the wedding approaches, you might also choose to write a welcome letter for your out-of-town guests who will be traveling to be there on your special day. This is a very thoughtful gesture, and visitors will be grateful for any information about the celebration (or even your favorite local restaurants), as well as lists of local attractions and transportation options.

line 3: vendors and service providers

When you're communicating with your wedding service providers, start by being prepared. Do as much research as you can about what services or products are available. Find out a bit about the company and how they work. And bring your thoughts and notes about what you want for the elements you're discussing, whether it's flowers, food, or formal invitations. You should also make sure you know what your budget is, and what the going rates are for these products and services.

Once you're ready to sign on the dotted line, make sure to have a written agreement for every service that lists all the details you're agreeing to, whether it's the number of hours provided by your photographer, the cost for your string trio for the ceremony, or your exact menu details. This advice applies to everything, from food to flowers, and music to transportation. If a vendor refuses to provide you with a written proposal and agreement outlining the goods and/or services they'll provide, along with their payment and cancellation policies, you should refuse to work with them, because they are likely not professional enough to entrust with your wedding.

Whenever you make changes to the written agreement, get those changes in writing as a revision or an addendum. And if you have a conference call where decisions (or promises) are made, ask for a recap in writing so that everyone is clear on all points.

On another note, don't be afraid to speak frankly with your wedding vendors. Share any concerns, problems, or issues you have, whether it's about a budget or design detail, a timing question, or a difficult family member. It's likely that they will have great solutions to offer, based on their experience in the field.

line 4: money talks

Money can be a stressful topic any day of the week. Weddings require money. Put the two together . . . you can see where this is going. The most important advice

When communicating with vendors and service providers, get details in writing. If you'll hire a vintage car, ask for the make and model, and what the backup plan is in case of a breakdown.

I can give you is to talk about money openly and honestly, with your fiancé, with your family or anyone else who is contributing to the celebration, and even with your vendors.

At the beginning of your process, talk about how you'll deal with finances related to the wedding. Be clear where the funds will come from, what your target budget is, and what your maximum spending might be.

Communication
DO'S & DON'TS

- **Do be audibly grateful.** It takes a village to put together a wedding. Let people know that you are thankful for their help—and let them know it often.

- **Don't be a boss.** Remember that this is a wedding, not an aerospace-engineering project. Resist the temptation to foist giant (even well-designed) spreadsheets or to-do lists on others. Assign tasks with tact and sensitivity, for the best results.

- **Do be a diplomat.** See both sides of any difficult situation. Really listen when your fiancé or family members are expressing concerns to you, and try to create compromises that work for all parties whenever possible. Build bridges rather than burning them.

- **Don't act entitled.** Everyone knows it's your special day/month/year, so avoid the impulse to remind them every time something rubs you the wrong way.

- **Do speak up.** If you take on too many tasks and become overwhelmed, and keep quiet about it for too long, you might have a bridal meltdown, triggered by something really unimportant. If something's bothering you, speak up, but do it politely and with other people's feelings and concerns in mind.

- **Don't freak out.** My experience has taught me that blowing up about things doesn't necessarily guarantee they'll get solved. Just yesterday we heard that some special glasses we ordered months ago for a wedding two days from now were discontinued. Rather than "flipping the switch," which seemed appropriate at the time, given the urgency of the situation, I decided to tell our rental company that I had every confidence two days was plenty of time for them to solve the problem. And wouldn't you know, this morning they called me and it's all better. There are very few things that can't be solved with a little time. And those that can't be solved won't be solved with tears or insults or hyperventilating. Sometimes you won't be so lucky and you will need a backup plan, but remember that melting down will not get you where you need to be. Some patience and a little bit of flexibility can often save the day.

Make sure that you and your fiancé understand each other's money-management styles, and be considerate of each other's thoughts and needs.

Your fiancé, for example, may not understand why it's necessary to have those letter-pressed invitations when you can order flat-printed versions for a fraction of the cost online. His family may want a big wedding, but your family may not be able (or willing) to pay for it. The point is, the more clarity you can have upfront, the less conflict you're apt to have. Wedding budgets can get out of control quickly, and surprises or expensive add-ons can be a source of stress between couples and families, so do whatever you can to avoid conflicts around money.

line 5:
wedding words

Of course you'll be talking all day at the wedding itself, and that's a time you should focus on sharing the love and happiness you feel with everyone around you. Forgive all small transgressions and embrace the moment.

If you decide you'd like to say a few words at the wedding reception, a good time to do that is at the beginning of the party, say, just before the meal is served, when you could welcome everyone, thank them for coming, and encourage them to have a wonderful time celebrating.

Another great opportunity is just after you cut the cake, when you can share a few thoughts about the happiness the day has brought you and thank those who made it possible. Don't forget to tell everyone how much you love your new husband!

One final note on speaking in front of your wedding crowd: If you're an emotional person, you might want to practice your planned thoughts in advance of the wedding day. I offer this advice from my own point of reference, having broken down myself at my sister's engagement party. I speak in public on a fairly regular basis, but the few heartfelt words I wanted to share with our friends and family just knocked me out and at this very important moment, I became a blubbering idiot, incapable of finishing a sentence. Be prepared.

the DRESS

finding it and wearing it well

What other single garment has more importance in a woman's life? What other outfit is dreamed about and imagined and loved as much? I can't think of one.

In the western world, brides now generally wear some shade of white, thanks to the trendsetting Queen Victoria, who, in 1840 decided to don a white lace gown to her own wedding, at a time when bold colors were more the fashion for brides. Seeing her portrait, brides around the world began copying her style, and the trend has now become a full-fledged tradition.

Choosing a dress is one of the most fun (yet sometimes stressful) parts of being a bride. Let's explore silhouettes, styles, and secrets to help you discover and dazzle in your own dream dress.

dress silhouettes

Dresses come in so many styles, with seemingly endless details and embellishments: beads, flowers, bows, buttons, even feathers. But perhaps the most important element of a wedding gown is its overall shape, or silhouette.

The lovely ladies at right, arranged in the atelier at The White Dress are representative of some classic and fresh dress styles. Check the Resource Guide for contact information. From left to right, here's a basic description:

"Newport" by Melissa Sweet is a Strapless "Fit-to-Flare" silhouette in silk shantung, with a neckline referred to as a "crumb catcher." An interesting detail at the bust is ideal for smaller brides, as it adds dimension to the chest.

"Tinsley" by Anne Barge is a classic A-line dress with a bateau neckline. The silk organza skirt is paired with a Chantilly lace bodice. In general, A-line silhouettes flatter almost every body type, as they accentuate the natural curves of a woman's body.

"Carrington" by Modern Trousseau combines a fabulous full ball skirt in tulle with a sweetheart neckline. A ball skirt silhouette can camouflage hips and help define the waist.

"Sage" by Augusta Jones is a modern sheath silhouette in silk charmeuse with a V-neckline. This body-hugging silhouette is best for slender brides.

"Ashten" by Augusta Jones combines the sheath shape with an Empire waist, in English net with metallic Chantilly lace. Empire silhouettes flatter petite brides.

selecting your wedding gown

My friend and colleague Beth Chapman owns a beautiful bridal boutique in Connecticut called The White Dress. It's set in an historic home near the shore, and she has created a lovely, relaxing environment where future brides are pampered and guided as they choose this most personal of garments—their wedding dress.

I've asked Beth to share some of her insider advice to help make this wonderful, but sometimes overwhelming, process easier and more fun.

- **Secure your wedding date and venue before you select a dress.** You'll choose a very different look for a summer beach wedding than for a fireside ceremony in an historic lodge. Let the season and setting of your celebration inspire you and help you choose fabrics, styles, and details that will work best.

- **Set a dress budget that includes the extras.** Remember, in addition to the gown itself, you'll need accessories (foundation garments, a veil or headpiece, jewelry, and shoes), alterations, and possibly gown cleaning and preservation after the wedding. Don't be afraid to share your budget with your salesperson. If they know your price range, they'll be able to help guide you toward your best choices.

- **Pick the right bridal store.** Research bridal retailers that carry designers you like. Bridal blogs are a great resource for reviews of service and selection.

Corset-style details are classically bridal, yet sexy as well. Choose a dress with a lace-up bodice, or wear a sultry corset under your gown as a surprise just for your groom.

If you are a department-store shopper, a larger bridal salon with a wide selection of gowns may be the right fit for you. If you prefer to browse in small boutiques, a more intimate bridal shop might be perfect for you.

Whether it's a delicate ribbon sash at your waist, a vintage-inspired brooch anchoring a bow, or a sweeping train, unique accents make the dress special. When you find your dress, you'll just know it's perfect for you.

- **Plan ahead, if you can.** Keep in mind that it can sometimes take four to six months to produce a wedding gown, and you'll need fittings and alterations once the gown comes in. If you have less time, don't panic. Just let your salesperson know your time frame and ask them for styles that will work with your needs.

- **Reflect your personal style, not the trends.** Your wedding day is not necessarily the best time to make a new fashion statement. Your gown should flatter your best physical assets, harmonize with the overall

mood of your celebration, and most important, make you feel wonderful. A good tip is to imagine yourself looking at your photos 10, even 20 years from now. Classic elegance never goes out of style.

- **Skip the entourage.** To streamline your shopping experience, bring only one or two people with you. Choose family or friends who know your style rather than bringing a big group. More opinions are not always better, and too many opinions can be confusing and stress-inducing.

- **Don't be alarmed by the size.** It's not you. Bridal-gown sizes are different from their ready-to-wear counterparts. In many cases, a wedding dress can be two sizes larger than what you would normally wear. Once you have selected your gown, the bridal salon will take your measurements. Those measurements will be compared to the designer's size chart and the appropriate size will be selected for you.

- **Tell it like it is.** Don't be afraid to express yourself if you don't like something. Who knows—maybe there's a modification that can be made to that almost-perfect gown to make it just right for you. That being said, keep an open mind if your salesperson suggests trying on a dress you might not have considered, even if you don't like how it looks on the hanger. You never know—it could be the gown of your dreams, and some hanger-challenged dresses really come alive on the body.

- **Know the deal.** Before purchasing your gown, be sure you understand the policies of the salon. Ask for details on the deposit, alterations, and whether or not you will receive a discount on bridesmaid dresses or accessories if you purchase a gown. Get everything in writing so there are no surprises.

hint

Keep in mind that, generally, a gown can be altered only up to two sizes. Even if you're planning on losing weight, it's best to go with your current size at the time you purchase the dress. You can alter it once you reach your weight-loss goal. Never order a gown based on the size that you "plan to be." That can be a costly and upsetting mistake.

- **Understand your alterations.** It will take time to tailor your gown to fit your body perfectly. Factor in enough time to allow for multiple adjustments—generally there are about three fittings that take place in the last few months and weeks before the wedding. Before your first alteration, make sure to get your shoes and undergarments, and bring them to the fitting.

Ask your wedding photographer to take a picture of your dress before you put it on. It will always remind you of those exciting moments right before you slipped it on for the ceremony!

wedding gowns start with a good foundation

Proper undergarments will truly make a difference in the fit of your gown. Wait until after you buy your dress, then take time to select the perfect pieces. Choose a shop that specializes in foundations so that you'll be sized correctly.

A TIP TO REMEMBER:

Select a bra or bustier that cannot be seen—from the front or from the back. Make sure if your bra has lace, texture, or boning, that none are visible through the dress fabric.

to preserve or not to preserve?

Although you may wear your wedding dress only once, it is a precious garment, so you'll want to have it properly cleaned and protected after the wedding (after all, your daughter or your best friend may wish to wear it one day!). Don't simply rely on your local dry cleaner. Instead, use a company that specializes in gown preservation. Experts recommend an anti-sugar cleaning treatment and a storage box made with acid-free materials. These steps will allow for maximum longevity of the fabric and minimize the possibility that it will discolor or deteriorate over time.

wearing an heirloom dress

If you're lucky enough to have an heirloom dress in your family, there are a number of ways to update the look to suit your own style.

- The first thing to do once you've tried it on is to take it to a qualified tailor who can help you with any alterations, such as shortening the hem or taking in the waist. Make sure you're working with someone who has experience dealing with older fabrics.

- If there is any damage to the garment, your tailor can also recommend a good cleaner to help try to remove stains, or she may be able to make adjustments or add an accent, such as a decorative trim, sash, or brooch, to cover small imperfections.

- If for some reason you cannot wear the gown (it doesn't fit, it's too damaged to save the whole garment, or you just don't like it as is), consider taking it apart and using elements to accent your own gown, ensemble, or celebration.

- Use lace or tulle from the dress to make a veil or sash.

- Show the fabric to your stationer or baker to help inspire a pattern on your invitation or cake.

- Remove the sleeves and have them fashioned into a

ERICA: Do a photo check.

Ask someone to take a picture of you in your gown in the days/weeks prior to the wedding. Sometimes in reworking a dress during alterations, elements can change and you might not notice it in the dressing-room mirror. In my case, I had a ribbon removed from the gown's bodice, which the seamstress replaced with extra lace. It looked great in person, but in my wedding photos the extra lace created an opaque line around my waist that looked somewhat like a panty line . . . horrifying!

little bolero jacket to wear to the rehearsal dinner.

- Have a satin wrap sewn from the skirt fabric and wear it around your shoulders at the ceremony.
- Take the dress to a tailor and find out if the style can be given a face-lift to express your personal style.

the NOT going-away outfit

Whatever happened to that beautiful, stylish tradition, wherein the bride would slip away at the reception and step into a wonderful suit or dress in preparation for the big send-off to the honeymoon? She'd emerge ready-to-travel in a super-cute outfit, as if she and her new husband couldn't wait to hop in that getaway car and start their new adventure together . . .

What happened is, brides and grooms don't leave anymore. In fact, they not only don't leave—they have after-parties that go on till all hours and next-day brunches, and I'm all for it! Recently I've noticed brides planning special outfits for these festivities. Typically for an after party, they're flirtier, shorter ensembles with bold accents and a little extra something-something. So why not take advantage of this fashion opportunity and change into a sassy little number for your late-night revelry?

ACCESSORIES

jewelry, shoes, flowers, and more

Antique diamond bracelets. Funky pendants. Vintage lace veils, cascading behind you. I've seen brides float down the aisle adorned with sparkly belts, red (and green and blue) suede shoes, feather-collared bouquets, and fresh flowers tucked into their locks. Thankfully, not all at once.

Whether you want a hint of sparkle, an accent, a modern touch, or a flash of glam, accessories allow you to personalize your look. And that's what it's all about. Choose accessories that complement your dress and express your own style.

veiled intentions

A veil is a classic bridal accessory, dating back to ancient times. Traditionally, a veil was worn covering the face for the ceremony, a symbol of purity and humility. Some also say it confused evil spirits, who couldn't get a good look at the bride on the way to the ceremony.

- Hindu and Muslim brides wear veils with their bridal outfits. The veil is made to match the wedding outfit, which is typically a traditional sari or *lengha*, and is seen as a symbol of bridal modesty.

- Western brides have many choices when it comes to wearing a veil—from short "blusher" lengths that come just to the chin or shoulders, to full-length, dramatic lace and tulle varieties, and everything in between. Veils don't necessarily even cover the face anymore. Some brides prefer to attach fabric to a hair comb and let it cascade behind them.

I am a huge fan of veils for the ceremony. Of course it depends on the bride and the gown and the setting, but there is just something, well—magical—about soft, ethereal fabric falling around a bride's glowing face as she floats down the aisle. Is a veil right for you?

Did you know?

In the Jewish tradition, just before the ceremony, the groom lifts the bride's veil to make sure he's got the right woman. Some say this tradition dates back to the Old Testament, when Jacob, who was set to marry Rachel, was tricked into marrying her sister Leah.

- If you're considering a veil, make sure you try it on with your dress and with any other accessories you're considering.

- Many brides wear a veil for the ceremony, then remove it before cocktail hour or the reception. This is a great idea, because it not only allows you to change up your look for the party, but removing the veil also allows for easier mingling and dancing.

A veil is certainly a fashion statement, but if you'll be married in a religious ceremony, wearing one can also be a way of showing respect if your dress shows bare shoulders or features a low-cut back. Before the reception you can remove the veil to reveal your sexier look.

B2B: veils

DEBBY: Veiled secrets.

Try on a veil with a blusher. I swore I wouldn't wear one—and then I tried one on. Oh my goodness! It transformed me into a romantic vision of a bride. I was just so much prettier from behind than thin gauzy fabric. I convinced a friend who was getting married to try a blusher veil on, and she had the exact same reaction I did. The blusher is powerful stuff. And the veil looks beautiful in my photos.

jewelry

Jewelry is such a personal declaration. I have seen brides wear big, statement pieces; delicate heirlooms; classic pearl bracelets; and big gem-studded cuffs. One groom presented his bride with a gorgeous diamond necklace that he had designed himself as a wedding gift.

What should you wear? The key is balance. The biggest mistakes you can make are wearing too many different pieces or wearing jewelry that competes with your dress.

Did you know?

Brides in India are some of the most beautifully jewel-bedecked creatures I have ever seen. They break out all the best jewelry, sometimes family heirlooms, sometimes pieces created just for them, and adorn themselves with gold bangles, dangling earrings, sparkling *bindis* (those lovely accents on their foreheads), and *maang tikka* (jeweled ornaments that are clipped into their hair).

The wedding ceremony itself often includes a moment when the groom's family gifts jewelry to the bride as a symbol of her joining the family.

What to do if your groom gives you jewelry as a wedding present? Wear it if at all possible. Chances are, he waited to give it to you because it's a really special piece, and he would likely be very proud if you showed it off on the big day.

Consider the following when you're choosing your wedding jewelry:

- **The neckline of the dress.** If it's a one-shoulder cut or has a high neck or other prominent details, you might want to skip a necklace and just go with great earrings.

- **The fabric.** Before you choose a fancy bangle for your wrist, make sure it won't catch on the lace or tulle in your dress while you're moving, mingling, and dancing.

- **The dress details.** If your dress features a lot of beadwork, ruching, embroidery, or other major accents, take a simpler approach to jewelry. Wear simple stud earrings and let the dress shine.

What bride doesn't like a little sparkle? Consider adding a wide jeweled cuff or a classic pearl bracelet (or three) to switch up your look just before the party.

Of course, you can feel free to wear red shoes to your ceremony, or you could save them, and a pair of dangly earrings, as accents for the reception. Create looks that reflect your true personal style throughout the celebration.

changing your look with accessories

If you like, you can switch up your style between the ceremony and the reception.

For the ceremony:

- Wear a demure little jacket or shawl and a pair of simple earrings.
- Cover your face and shoulders with a beautiful veil, and keep makeup light and fresh.
- Carry a vintage handkerchief tied loosely around your bouquet in case of tears.
- Add feathers or crystals or trailing ribbons to your bouquet.
- Wear gloves.
- Pin fresh flowers in your hair.

Switch it up for the reception:

- Bustle up your dress train (if applicable).
- Remove your veil.
- Add a deeper lip color or a bit more eye makeup.
- Add a sash or sparkly belt or brooch to a simple dress.
- Add a statement necklace or dramatic earrings, if they work with your dress.
- Change into a pair of glamorous red shoes.

bridal shoes

So many brides tell me in advance of the wedding that they don't care if their feet kill them—they're wearing that fabulous pair of stilettos that look so perfect with the dress. *No matter what.* I always say, that's great, but let's have a Plan B, just in case. And let's just say that Plan B often goes into effect by about an hour and a half into the reception.

No matter what, you should plan for a shoe change, and remember that the height of your shoe and the length of your dress are obviously related. Take any and all shoes you plan on wearing with you to your dress fittings so you can discuss options with your seamstress. My advice is to skip the sky-high heels altogether (even though I love wearing them myself), and opt for a more moderate heel, as your first choice, so that if you have to switch to a slightly lower heel, you're not ruining the look of the dress. And chances are greater if you start out in a bit more comfort, you might not have to change at all.

Did you know?

The Jimmy Choo toss. Yes, that's right, ladies. Before the bouquet became the coveted hurled item of choice at receptions, brides used to toss their pumps over their shoulder for one lucky gal to catch. It was a shoe-in that she'd be the next to marry!

Make sure to test your wedding shoes out for any issues and scuff the bottoms with a nail file before wearing them down the aisle and onto the dance floor. And don't forget to get a photo of them for the memory book!

bridesmaid accessories: less is more

I was having dinner with some girlfriends in a beautiful old hotel in Europe recently, and my sister came back from the ladies' room saying that there was a wedding going on downstairs in the ballroom. She knew this because eight of the bridesmaids were in the bathroom together complaining about how uncomfortable their shoes were and how much they hated their dresses and jewelry. My sister dragged me back downstairs and I could see that their complaints were not unwarranted.

These pretty girls were so overdone, they actually looked *costumed*. In her attempt to let her beautiful, old-world venue influence her bridesmaids' attire, the bride had overshot her mark by, well, by a long shot. The dresses were a bold emerald green, accented with giant emerald-green fabric flowers, and the young ladies were all wearing huge necklaces. Although I am generally known for saying, "Any look is better than no look at all," this was just honestly "too much look."

Remember that bridesmaids have their pretty dresses and flowers as accents for the ceremony. They may not need anything more. For the reception, a few pretty bangles or a simple necklace may be the perfect festive addition.

The lesson here is that the simple stunning principle applies to accessories, as well as to almost everything else. If your bridesmaid dresses are very plain, you might be able to get away with some striking earrings or a stack of bangles. If, however, the dresses have a lot going on, such as a bold print or a one-shoulder cut or other architectural design, ease up on the accessories and let the fashion shine.

DANCING FEET

Having witnessed many a poor maid taping up blisters and switching to flip-flops mid-reception, I have come up with a good idea to avoid rubbing bridesmaid feet the wrong way. I suggest that the bride wear a pair of the proposed bridesmaid shoes in a test run for exactly the number of hours her maids will be on their feet on the big day. If said bride makes it through with no issues, she can ask her ladies to follow in her footsteps.

FLOWERS ARE ACCESSORIES TOO

When you're planning your outfit and your bridesmaid ensembles, keep your floral choices in mind. The florist's term for bouquets is "personal flowers"—and they should be personal.

In general, I am in favor of smaller "posies" or even single blossoms for bridesmaids—they are chic, easy to carry, and budget-friendly. Of course, if you prefer something more dramatic, that's fine, too. And if you're not a super-flowery bride, you shouldn't feel pressured to have the ladies carry flowers at all. After

As the bride, you should determine what your bouquet will look like first, then design the maids' flowers to coordinate. Will you carry an ethereal white bouquet or one that is rich with color?

all, the tradition of bridesmaid bouquets comes from those less hygienic days when the fragrance from flowers was used to cover up body odors. I'm confident that's not going to be a factor now . . .

As the bride, you should carry blossoms that reflect who you are. You can make a bold statement by complementing your dress with a vibrant bouquet in reds, hot pinks, or another dramatic hue. You can create a vintage look by wrapping the stems with lace or ribbon streamers.

If you're working with a floral designer, make sure to show him a picture of your dress, front and back. If possible, share photos of any accessories you're planning to wear, such as a veil or bracelet. He should also know about the look and feel of your ceremony and reception (colors, fabrics, décor, etc.). It will help him design a beautiful bouquet to harmonize with your look.

old, new, borrowed, blue

I love this tradition. One lucky bride I know got to "borrow" an enormous blue sapphire ring. Another carried an "old" family Bible down the aisle. New is easy—your shoes will do! Embrace these little details, and look for clever ways to incorporate them into your bridal attire.

Bridal Accessory DO'S & DON'TS

- **Do** choose your accessories to complement your dress. If the dress features elaborate embroidery or beading, let it shine and opt for simple earrings as your only accent. If the dress is very simple, wearing a statement piece (a beautiful necklace, for example) can add magic to your outfit.

- **Don't** wear your engagement ring on your ring finger for the ceremony. Either switch the ring to your right hand, or take it off for a few hours and put it back on top of the wedding band before the reception. If you choose the latter, you should definitely keep it in a safe place!

- **Do** change your accessories between the ceremony and reception, if you like. You can add a dramatic bracelet or necklace or a beautiful flower in your hair as a way to intensify your outfit as the party ramps up.

- **Don't** forget to consider your whole look. Your hair and makeup are also accessories, so if you'll go with a bold lip or nail color, keep other accents simple.

- **Do** wear heirloom pieces if you have them. Wouldn't it be wonderful to be photographed in the same necklace or earrings your mother and grandmother wore? If you don't have an heirloom tradition, consider starting one. Save your wedding jewelry and pass it on to another bride in your family or circle of friends.

FITNESS
expert advice for the wedding and beyond

Being a bride is about feeling beautiful, about celebrating and being celebrated, and about looking and being your best self. It's seen as an ideal day in a woman's life, a day for her beauty to shine and be admired. But with all the books, magazines, websites, and TV shows that urge rock-hard abs, toned arms, endless sex appeal, and everything in between, the pressure can really get to a girl.

I've spoken to my good friend, Sean Green, a former NBA player and current triathlete and coach, who also happens to be a trainer to more celebrities than I can list here. We talked about his top 10 tips for achieving your goals for bridal fitness and beyond. I've added some of my own thoughts, too.

the shape of your life

I can't tell you how many brides I've met who are waiting to shop for their wedding dress till they lose more weight, or how many are worrying about looking better. They'll do almost anything to make sure they attain their goals for this one big day, including skipping meals, working out excessively, and buying their dress in a smaller size to encourage weight loss.

It's great to meet a goal, and of course you want to feel lovely in your dress, but these extreme efforts, when not paired with a long-term lifestyle adjustment, can often result in more weight gain after the wedding when the pressure's off.

Your engagement is a wonderful beginning, a period that will lead to your new life with the person you love. Instead of making your wedding day a target, why not make this the beginning of a truly healthy lifestyle for you both?

Take a look at Sean's expert tips, and heed his words of wisdom on short-term results and long-term success.

With your new life about to begin, consider making lifestyle changes you can incorporate now and continue into the future. Become more active, get to know good ingredients, and take time to commune with nature and relax!

TIP 1

Sean says: Most important—get in shape for your life, not for your wedding. Your extra efforts to look good on the big day itself will certainly be appreciated, but how will you sustain your results after you get hitched? Have you thought about what happens after the wedding? Fitness should be incorporated into your lifestyle for the long term, and there's no better time to start than right now, with your goals, and your future good health, in mind.

Karen says: Set realistic targets for small changes you can live with long-term, like eating healthy six days a week, then giving yourself a day to cheat, and starting an exercise program that has variety and fits your schedule so you'll stay interested. I recently heard a story from a colleague who works in a wedding dress boutique. She said it's incredible how many women whittle away to nothing before the wedding, then come back six months after the big day to pick up their preserved gowns, having gained all the weight back. Don't let this be you!

TIP 2

Sean says: Fad restriction diets don't work! Although a severely restricted diet might give quick results, you'll gain the weight back right after you start eating normally again. Instead, eat whole foods, such as organic fruits and vegetables. Limit your intake of processed foods, and read labels—a general rule is that the shorter an ingredient list is, the better it is, so skip

products with ingredients you cannot pronounce. Shop on the perimeter of the grocery store—that's where all the fresh stuff is.

Karen says: If you need a way to jump-start your healthy diet, try a week of eating only home-prepared meals—no chips or frozen foods or takeout. Make a smoothie for breakfast with almond milk and fresh berries, whip up your own salad dressing and bring it for lunch, try miso soup or a handful of almonds as a snack, and steam up fresh fish and greens for dinner. Not only will you save calories—you'll save money, too, and you'll be feeling so great you'll want to do it again for another week!

TIP 3

Sean says: Try a low-glycemic diet. Stay away from white flour and processed sugars, and limit empty calories like soda, some sports drinks, and alcohol. Although many of us enjoy a glass of wine or a cocktail from time to time, there are experts who believe that alcohol and other foods with a high-glycemic index trigger blood-sugar swings that can cause your body to store fat.

Karen says: Alcohol can also make you eat more. As you get more relaxed, your willpower can relax, too. If you're focused on losing weight, have a glass of club soda with lemon or a cup of green tea. If you do drink occasionally, stick to light beer or a glass of wine, and avoid sugary mixers found in margaritas, mojitos, and other sweet cocktails.

SWEETEN THE DEAL

When you need a sweetener, try low-glycemic-index agave syrup—you can use it in cocktails and tea, on pancakes or over fruit, in sauces and curries—almost anywhere. It's available at many national chains, like Whole Foods, and health food stores everywhere.

TIP 4

Sean says: Never let yourself get thirsty. Many times, dehydration is misinterpreted as hunger. Staying well hydrated throughout your day, and especially when you're exercising, will help you regulate your appetite, improve your skin, and flush toxins out of your system.

Karen says: Find the amount of water that's right for you. If you can't deal with downing eight glasses a day, start with four. Maybe you can work your way up to seven. Small steps are a better way to ensure long-term success!

TIP 5

Sean says: Never let yourself get hungry. When we are ravenously hungry, we tend to overeat. Depending on your height and weight, your calorie needs will vary, but rather than eating two or three big meals and snacking all day, try breaking up your daily calories into six smaller meals.

Karen says: Those six smaller meals will likely also be easier on your digestion than three huge meals, making you feel lighter and more energetic throughout your day. Give it a try!

TIP 6

Sean says: Don't eat your biggest meal late in the day. As I tell all my clients, try to eat breakfast like a queen, lunch like a princess, and dinner like a handmaid. By eating your biggest meal earlier in the day, your body has time to burn off more calories while you're most active.

Karen says: This advice changed my life. If you're not a big breakfast person, don't worry. Just ease into the day with a "princessy" breakfast, then have a queen's lunch, and keep dinner light. You'll sleep better and feel better the next morning.

TIP 7

Sean says: Burn more than you consume. If you are not an avid gym-goer, head outdoors and walk, run, hike . . . play with the dog. Get a pedometer and try for a few more steps each day. The bottom line is that there is a certain number of calories that your body needs to keep it functioning every day. If you take in more than that, you'll put on weight. Weight loss is about the deficit between calories consumed and calories burned.

Karen says: Exercise isn't just a way to burn calories. It's a stress reliever, and every bride can use all the help she can get with alleviating stress. Instead of thinking of exercise as a chore or a bore, think of it as a chance to get out in nature, to learn a new skill, or just to clear your head. Even a short workout a few times a week will make a difference.

TIP 8

Sean says: A colorful plate is a healthier plate. When you're designing a meal, make sure it's full of a mix of colorful vegetables, brown whole grains, and vibrant greens, plus lean proteins.

Karen says: When it comes to putting together a healthy diet, a neutral color palette is always "out," and the more colors on your plate, the better! Remember that fruits and vegetables of different colors offer different vitamins and minerals.

TIP 9

Sean says: Add some lean muscle to your frame. When I say "add lean muscle," I don't mean that you should bulk up. When you incorporate strength training into your workouts, such as lifting light weights consistently, you develop lean muscle. The difference is that one pound of lean muscle burns roughly 40–50 calories a day, while a pound of fat burns only about 2–5 calories daily. You do the math.

Karen says: As if the above weren't enough to convince you, how about this? Your arms will look fabulous in your dress and you'll feel stronger, sexier, and more confident.

TIP 10

Sean says: Watch that number . . . but not your weight. I work with so many women who are obsessed with how much they weigh, and I'm here to tell you this is the wrong approach. The number you should be watching is your body-fat percentage. The fact is that even if you are not overweight, you can be "over-fat." And the opposite is true as well—you can weigh more, but be lean and lovely.

Karen says: Check with your doctor or a fitness professional to have your body fat measured, and find out what your target should be. And be sure to talk to your doctor before starting your new fitness plan. She can help you make sure you're on the right track toward a lifetime of healthy practices.

sweating it one on one?

Are you and your future husband well matched athletically? If so, plan to share a couple of workouts a week—running, shooting hoops, playing tennis, swimming. You'll keep each other motivated, get a chance to

Dancing together is a great way to share a healthy activity that is also romantic and fun. So go ahead, grab your partner by the hand.

extra!

CRUNCHES FOR A TIME-CRUNCHED BRIDE?

Whether your wedding is coming up quickly or you just don't have a lot of time to devote to workouts, Sean has a solution. He recommends short, highly intense 30-minute workouts. They keep you interested and they don't beat your body up as much as a longer session might, plus they give you more recovery time so you'll be ready for another 30 minutes the next day. Try a 10-minute cardio warm-up, 10 minutes of strength training (target a different area each day), and finish with 10 more minutes of cardio (dancing, jumping rope, running). And of course, don't forget to stretch and stay hydrated!

spend some fun time together, and reap the benefits of healthier bodies and minds!

If your routines or preferences aren't in sync for regular workouts, look for ways you can spend some active time with your fiancé—taking a walk around town or hiking in the country or going dancing together (how about some lessons for that big first dance?). These are all great ways to burn off calories and enjoy each other at the same time. Salsa anyone?

BEAUTY
celebrity artists
share their secrets

How do you envision your look for the big day? Will your skin be soft and dewy with just a hint of color? Will you have smoky eyes or pouty red lips? Will your hair be swept back into an elegant chignon or flowing in waves over your shoulders?

Chances are you're already thinking about how you want to wear your hair and makeup for the wedding, and how to best take care of your skin. Maybe you've looked online for ideas or cut photos that inspired you out of magazines. That's great. But whether you'll choose to hire professionals to style your hair and makeup for the big day or you'll do it yourself, take a look at the great advice on these pages from some of my favorite celebrity makeup and hair gurus. They'll help you pare down the fluff and think about what you need. I've also included some tips for nurturing your inner beauty along the way, to enhance that bridal glow from within!

making up

Unless you are a makeup professional or a talented amateur, I highly recommend hiring an expert to help you look your best on your wedding day. Even if you want a simple, natural look, a professional makeup artist can bring out your most beautiful features, and will help you look your best in your photos, which—don't forget—last forever.

I also suggest paying for a makeup trial with your chosen pro in advance of the wedding, so that you and your artist can agree on your look. At the trial, you can take photos of your makeup and write down shades to be sure you get exactly what you want.

If you do decide to do your own makeup, be sure to do a trial on yourself at least once or twice, keeping in mind your dress and accessories. Ask a friend to take a picture so you can confirm you're happy with your work.

To help you achieve your own simple stunning look, I asked my friend, celebrity makeup artist Jacqueline Phillips, who not only works with the stars but also styles brides for weddings, to give us her top five tips for bridal makeup.

In my experience, hair and makeup are the one topic that seems to stress brides out the most in the days leading up to the wedding. Communicate what you want as clearly as possible when you're talking with your hair and makeup pros and you'll have a much smoother path to looking and feeling great.

extra!

PLAN YOUR TOTAL LOOK.

If you're working with the same person for hair and makeup, try both looks together. If not, make sure to bring photos of your chosen styles for each to show the other artist. Also bring pictures of your dress, as well as any accessories you're considering (necklace, hair clip, veil). A neckline detail on your gown, for example, might influence whether you wear your hair cascading over your shoulders or in a sleek upsweep.

TIP 1

Jacqui says: Look like you, only better. In other words, plan to enhance and play up your own great attributes, rather than trying to look like someone else. Too many brides have a "one-day-only" or "celebrity" look in mind that doesn't suit their style, personality, or features. If you're not someone who wears a lot of makeup normally, for example, you probably shouldn't opt for high-drama eye shadow and loads of lipstick. Instead, highlight your best features and celebrate your own personal beauty.

TIP 2

Jacqui says: Find pictures of looks you like. I always ask brides to flip through magazines and tear out pages

of looks that appeal to them and bring those pictures to our first meeting. If you like the eye makeup featured on one actress or model and the lip color on another, save both pages. The goal is to have a collective idea of what you want your look to be on your wedding day. You should also feel free to pull out photos of looks you don't like. Once your makeup artist has an idea of what you're envisioning, he or she can evaluate what will work on you and advise you on how to combine elements for the best result.

TIP 3

Jacqui says: **Choose your focus.** It's important to choose which attribute on your face you want to highlight especially. Do you want your eyes, lips, or skin to be your most prominent feature? How would you like your skin to look? Dewy, satiny, matte, or shimmering? Just like editing your accessories, you'll want to edit your makeup choices to make sure your overall look is not overdone.

TIP 4

Jacqui says: **Experience counts.** Hire hair and makeup pros who have styled numerous brides. Check out their websites and/or portfolios, chat with them on the phone, meet them in person, and check their references. Are they on time and organized? Also, it's important to have a warm rapport with your hair and makeup team—you'll be spending part of your wedding day with them, after all, so you'll want to make sure

tip

Worried about drinking red wine at the wedding for fear of stained teeth? I have heard that from many a bride. So I asked dentist-to-the-stars Marc Lowenberg if there was any solution for a wine-loving bride other than sipping Barolo through a straw (unacceptable!). He suggests rubbing just a little Vaseline on your teeth before you imbibe. It might not taste great, but it will form a protective covering over the teeth and the wine will roll right off. Hey, it also makes your pearly whites even glossier than usual.

their energy works with yours and your personalities are well matched.

TIP 5

Jacqui says: **Don't be afraid to speak up.** If you are not happy with your makeup or hair trials, keep trying until you're not just satisfied, but delighted. Your styling pros should have no problems taking direction from

Consider what your makeup needs will be on the big day. If there's a big break between your ceremony and reception, or if you're expecting really hot weather, you may wish to have your makeup artist stay to do touchups before your portraits.

you, and they should be eager to create the look you want. If they are not responsive or are just not getting it, it might be worth choosing another salon or artist.

skin-care

If you don't already have a skin-care routine in place, what better time to start creating one than now? If your skin is healthy and in good shape, just add in regular exfoliation and use a moisturizer with sunscreen on your face, neck, hands, and chest. You'll thank me later . . .

If you have skin issues, I suggest you start by visiting a good dermatologist for an overall skin exam. She'll be able to tell you what kind of skin you have, and she might be able to advise you on what products or medications can help make your skin more healthy.

You also might want to consider making an appointment for a series of regular facials. Aside from being a great way to pamper yourself, a regular routine of deep exfoliation and moisture, along with masks or other treatments designed for your skin type, can really improve the health of your skin.

Talk to your doctor about whether you should add vitamin supplements to your daily routine as well, and don't forget to drink plenty of water.

Facials are a way of killing two birds with one stone. First, you're taking care of your skin in preparation for the celebration. Second, you're pampering yourself. Enjoy!

hint

If you find you have a pimple with any swelling or redness on the big day (or any day!), try this tip. Put a few eye drops (I use Visine) directly on the pimple. I'm telling you, it works for me, but of course try it out for yourself before the wedding, just to be safe.

a brush with celebrity

Hair is one of a bride's greatest accessories. Whether it's short and sassy or long and lustrous, your hairstyle should reflect your personal style and should harmonize with your outfit and accessories.

Vincent Roppatte, creative director of the salon at Saks Fifth Avenue in New York, styles socialites, superstars, and media luminaries. He offers some excellent advice for your big day.

TIP 1

Vincent says: Choose your wedding gown before deciding on your hairstyle. If you know you'll want to wear your hair down for your wedding day, take that into account when looking for your gown. If the dress is very formal, a soft, romantic updo may be just the ticket. If the dress is simpler, cascades of flowing hair around your face may complement it perfectly.

Did you know?

It's considered good luck for a bride to glance at herself in the mirror just before leaving for the ceremony. So go ahead, take one last look at your gorgeous self!

TIP 2

Vincent says: Go through a trial run with your stylist at least a month before the wedding. Bring any hair accessories you'd like to try—combs, veil, tiara—so that you can work with them and see how best to accent your look. Don't forget to take photos of your chosen look for your reference.

TIP 3

Vincent says: Don't be afraid to experiment with your style. You're marrying the love of your life, not your same old do. There are so many wonderful products available now—extensions, for example—that can add volume and drama to your wedding day style. Give them a try and see what works.

TIP 4

Vincent says: Consider the health and shine of your hair. If your hair is brittle or in less than great condition, allow yourself a few months to get it healthy. Brush regularly, use conditioners recommended by

When you're thinking about how to wear your hair, consider how you feel most beautiful, and how you'll be most comfortable. For example: if the weather will be warm or if you plan to dance all night (of course you do!), you might want a style that pulls at least part of your hair away from your face.

your trusted stylist, and if you color your hair, make sure to have it done one to two weeks before the wedding so it will look its best.

TIP 5

Vincent says: Don't use any chemicals on your hair (straighteners, permanent wave chemicals, etc.) too close to the wedding day. Your stylist can help you achieve the look you want for the big day without risking any big surprises or allergic reactions.

TIP 6

Vincent says: Don't over-condition your hair the night before the wedding. Hair that's too clean or too well conditioned doesn't absorb styling products well and can be limp or hard to control.

TIP 7

Vincent says: If your hair stylist happens to be very dear to you, why not invite him to the wedding? Not only will he be there to celebrate with you—he'll also likely not mind helping with quick fixes or touch ups when you need them.

If you take one piece of advice from this book, make it this one: take a few moments each day to just be peaceful. I promise, making quiet time a part of your routine will pay off during your wedding planning process and way beyond.

inner beauty

Throughout your engagement, take time to reflect and nurture your inner self as well as your physical self. Try some of these techniques for alleviating stress and enhancing your own sense of peace and well-being during this busy, emotional time.

- **Find a quiet space.** Make a little time each day, early in the morning or just before bed, to sit quietly and reflect. Light a candle, sip a cup of tea, and focus on clearing your mind. Lots of brides tell me they have trouble falling asleep because they're worried about details. You can try spending a few minutes every night before bed actively *not* thinking about the wedding. Instead, envision something peaceful, like the ocean or a field of flowers or a happy memory.

- **Try yoga.** You will be surprised how this incredible workout can add peace and calm to your daily life. If you can't make time for yoga, add some slow stretches to your routine before bed or when you first awake.

- **Keep a journal.** Write down your feelings— describe your excitement, document the happy moments you're sharing, even your hopes, fears, and concerns. Getting it down on paper not only makes for beautiful memories—it can also be a way of organizing your thoughts, not to mention getting stress off your chest and on to the page.

Take deep breaths. Experts agree. Inhaling deeply and breathing out slowly can have an almost instant calming effect on you. Try breathing in to a slow count of four, then exhaling to a count of eight. Repeat this whenever you need a refreshing lift.

Do *you* time. If you don't like journaling or yoga's just not your thing, do whatever works for you. Jump on your bed and listen to rock music or take a kick-boxing class—the point is to take time for yourself to help relieve stress and stay healthy.

bridal beauty
DO'S & DON'TS

- **Do** allow plenty of time for hair and makeup on your wedding day. An hour for makeup and an hour for hair is a good estimate, but build a little time around both so that you won't feel rushed. Also keep in mind whether you'll have to travel to and from a salon.

- **Don't** be too trendy. Even fashionista brides will regret choosing the latest and greatest look one year, or 10 years, down the line. Skip what's on the runway now and consider timeless style for inspiration, with accent details that add a modern twist.

- **Do** provide hair and makeup services for your attendants if you require them to wear a certain look. Otherwise, you're not obligated, but it's certainly a nice touch.

- **Don't** over-tan. In case you haven't heard, sun-worshipping will damage your skin. If you feel you need a little extra glow, consider a professionally applied airbrush tan, and have it done a day or two before the wedding. But make sure to do a trial run a few weeks in advance so you know what to expect!

- **Do** consider having your hair and makeup artists come to you where you'll be getting ready on the wedding day. Stylists who specialize in weddings often offer this service, and it's so much nicer than running back and forth between salons. Of course, it's less expensive to go to the salon, as you're not pulling the artist out for hours at a time, but if you opt to go to them, be sure to allow even more time for travel, and bring a silk scarf to protect your hair on the way home.

- **Don't** forget to bring a "cosmetic update" kit with you to the wedding. Fill a small purse with your lip gloss, eye liner, a stain-removing pen, and anything else you might need.

- **Do** designate a special lady to be your "makeup fairy" at the festivities. Her job is to tell you when you need a touch-up.

here comes THE BRIDE
wisdom for your wedding day

When you wake up that morning, on the day you will be married, take a moment to consider how lucky you are. You are truly blessed to have chosen—and to have been chosen by—a partner who loves you and wants to build a life together with you. That alone is a rare and wonderful notion, isn't it? Take a deep breath, look out the window, and appreciate everything about this magical moment. Look in the mirror—yes, it's your day!

It doesn't matter if the sky is perfectly clear or the temperature is just right. After all, your heart is full of hope and happiness, and that is as just right as just right can be. What really matters is that you are loved by someone incredibly special, and you are loved by those who are there to share in this moment. What really matters is that your life is about to change in beautiful ways. Reflect on this sweet step toward a new, exciting journey. Celebrate your femininity, your romantic self, and your possibilities and dreams. Celebrate your family and your friends. Celebrate you!

practically speaking

Okay, we're all feeling romantic and dreamy after that introduction, right? But there are plenty of details that will help to make sure you're free to enjoy your wedding.

If you're planning to stay in a hotel on your wedding night, consider reserving that room (or another less expensive room) for the night before the wedding. You'll have everything you need with you, and instead of worrying about getting around, you'll be able to relax, reflect, and get ready without rushing. If you've opted for the less-expensive room for that extra night, remind the front desk that you're about to be a bride and ask if it's possible to upgrade when you check in. Hey, Squeaky Wheel, you never know.

- **Eat before the ceremony.** Even if it's just a simple lunch, plan to have something healthy, light, and delicious so that you'll feel energized for all the festivities. I've seen too many brides avoid eating or just forget to grab something. Inevitably they feel tired or faint during the reception, especially after a glass or two of champagne.

Take a few quiet moments before or after the ceremony to be alone and savor the sweetness of your love.

- **Make someone else your point person on the day of the wedding.** Hire someone or choose a trusted friend or family member who is not in your bridal party. No one should call you on the big day unless it's an emergency. Review all important details with your chosen contact before the big day, and then let it all go and let her take care of it.

- **If you'll be photographed before the ceremony, ask your photographer to arrange a first meeting for you and your groom, alone, somewhere quiet and special.** This moment will give your fiancé a chance to marvel at your beauty up close, and for you both to exchange a few words.

- **Pack a bridal emergency kit.** Include pain relievers, a sewing kit, safety pins, breath mints, bobby pins, tissues, double-stick fashion tape, comfortable flat shoes, and a small flask full of whiskey (just kidding about that last part, unless you really like whiskey).

- **Assign someone to be in charge of moving gifts and personal items from the reception.** You don't want to be organizing or hauling stuff around after the high of your celebration. Weeks before the big day, pick a responsible friend or member of your family and ask them to coordinate getting everything back to your house or in your parents' car, for example. It's really not a good idea to save this request for the last minute, since your guests may have other responsibilities to take care of.

blissfully speaking

- **On your wedding morning, take a moment to write a note to your fiancé.** Have your maid of honor or another friend deliver it to him before you see each other and tell him everything you're feeling. Better yet, decide in advance that each of you will write a letter to the other, which you'll seal in envelopes. Don't open them. Instead, wait until your first anniversary. Then read them aloud over cake and champagne.

- **Spend part of your day in quiet reflection.** Even if it's only for a few minutes, take time to take it all in.

- **Do something you love.** Go swimming. Take a leisurely run in the park. Look at old photos. Watch a favorite movie. Relax and enjoy.

- **Get a massage.** So many brides tell me this is one thing they wish they had splurged for. You'll feel fabulous, your skin will glow, and you'll float down the aisle.

- **Thank your bridal party.** Take time with them individually or have a toast as you gather before the ceremony, and just let them know how much their support means to you.

- **Focus on happiness.** Forget about all the little worries you've had. Just let it all go—I promise it doesn't matter. Ignore anyone who isn't acting nice. Live right now, in this sweet, joyful moment!

photographically speaking: how to look great in your pictures

What I have noticed in the hundreds of weddings I've planned and designed, is that the best photos are not of the prettiest people. They are of the happiest people— people who are truly caught up in the excitement of their wedding day. Beyond that, here are few simple stunning tips for making the most of your wedding memories.

- **Take your portraits before the ceremony.** Although I know some couples don't want to see each other before the ceremony, the fact is, from a photographic standpoint, it's a great idea to take formal portraits when you're freshly pressed and coiffed. This is also a nice time to get some candid images of the two of you alone—on a rooftop, in a park, on a cobble-

> **tip**
> Even if it's raining outdoors, you may be able to take advantage of some soft natural light by taking pictures next to a window, where light will come in from the side and create a romantic mood.

stone street, or on a beautiful staircase. As mentioned before, if you're worried you'll ruin the surprise of seeing each other, arrange a time to meet alone before your portraits, when you're both dressed in your finery and getting excited—such a romantic moment!

- **Know your lighting.** If you like sunny portraits and shots of you and your sweetheart under a blue sky, make sure you plan for this when talking with your photographer. This even applies to décor photography—flowers and other details often photograph better in natural light. Night-time shots will add atmosphere and show the mood of your space.

- **Give your photographer a shot list.** This doesn't have to be a comprehensive list. Focus on the most important pictures and what kind of spirit or mood you hope to capture.

- **Forget the camera is there.** I know it's hard to do this when the bridal party is lined up for portraits, but try to let go, relax, and just enjoy the moment. If you need a little help, think of the moment your groom proposed or a happy walk on the beach you shared. This will translate to beautiful photos—I promise!

Find a beautiful window and have your photographer take a picture of you from all angles. You'll want to preserve the memory of your dress details, and a window provides a lovely, light-filled backdrop for these hopeful moments just before the ceremony.

B2B

inspiration and insight from real brides

I love hearing from real brides about their experiences. I could talk about weddings all day (and I often do!). In preparation for this book about brides, I decided to pose a whole bunch of questions to former brides, and I was amazed by how many insightful answers I received.

Though previous chapters have been peppered with pertinent thoughts from smart, savvy brides, there were just so many great tidbits and suggestions left over that I decided to make a special chapter out of the rest of the good advice. Of course every bride's experience is unique, but I hope a word or two from these ladies will resonate with you and offer you help or guidance as you make your way to your own big day.

Is there anything about your wedding you wish you had done differently?

ERICA: Listen live.

I wish we had listened to the band play in person instead of only calling their references.

DEBBY: Take it outside.

I would have had our bridal-party photos taken outside instead of inside our venue. Natural light would've been so much better.

ELAINE: Invite 'em all.

I wish I could have invited some extended family to the ceremony itself (we limited it to immediate family).

What's one thing you learned that you'd like to share?

LINDSAY: Do *you*.

Be true to yourselves as a couple. You only get to plan your wedding once, so make sure your celebration is a reflection of you and your future husband. It's important for you to be able to look back on your wedding day and say, "That's exactly the way we wanted it. That was us."

On the big day, forget everything except your happiness. Nothing else even comes close to mattering. Put on the dress, get pampered and fussed over, and prepare for the best ride of your life.

KATE: Get it on tape.

Hire a videographer. It was hands-down the best investment we made. We absolutely love our wedding video, and so do all of our family members. We thought videography was "cheesy," but a friend convinced us to go for it, and I am *so* glad we did. We cry every time we watch it together.

CINDY: Add personal touches.

It was amazing how small, handcrafted elements added magic to our wedding. At the suggestion of a close friend, we wrote personal notes to each guest telling each how important they were to us and how happy we were to share this day with them. We tucked the notes into envelopes and set them out at each guest's place setting.

JENNIFER: Go solo.

Although many brides may think this sounds strange, I purposefully spent the whole morning of the wedding day by myself. After having been busy the week leading up to the wedding—running around doing last-minute planning and hosting out-of-town family and friends— I needed some "me" time to relax, unwind, and quietly savor the excitement of the day.

DANA: Hire the best.

Pick vendors you absolutely trust. The level of stress will be so much lower if you're not worried if the flowers will look right, if the cake will taste good, or if the band will show up.

What was your favorite moment from the big day?

LINDSAY: Heart and soul.

Walking down the aisle toward my future husband while the Harlem Gospel Choir sang Sam Cooke's "You Send Me." That beautiful, soulful singing and the look of joy on my fiancé's face took my breath away.

DEBBY: Private party.

The 10 minutes after the ceremony when my husband and I were alone. I had thought we would drink some champagne, eat some hors d'oeuvres, and compare notes on the ceremony. Instead, he burst into tears that he had been barely holding back during the ceremony. He held me tight in his arms and told me how much the day meant to him. *Then* we had champagne and hors d'oeuvres. It was amazing! It was actually hard to leave that intimate moment to join all our friends and family for our cocktail hour.

ELAINE: The view from love.

The moment I remember most at the reception was sitting quietly with my new hubby at our single, beautiful candlelit dinner table and realizing that we could enjoy the moment and our families without having to enter-

tain a large number of guests. The day was truly just about making a commitment to one another and having our closest family bear witness to that.

KATE: Make memories.

A friend advised me to take mental snapshots throughout the day so that I would be sure to remember the special moments, and I would highly recommend this. For example, when I finally turned and looked at all of our guests during the ceremony, I took a mental snapshot of the way they looked and the beautiful setting—their faces, their clothes, the sky, and weather.

KATE: A walk with mom.

The walk down the aisle. My mom walked with me, since my father is deceased. I loved the feeling of being on my mom's arm and I could sense the love of family and friends surrounding me as they watched us make our way. I felt so beautiful and was so happy that the moment had come. As I walked, I looked straight into my groom's eyes the entire time. Right before my mom handed me over to my groom, she gave me a kiss on the cheek and whispered a sweet phrase from my childhood. It was a very loving moment.

DANA: An unexpected toast.

One of the highlights of my wedding day was my husband's speech. I hadn't heard it beforehand, so it was a surprise to me. It was sincere and heartfelt, with a mix of humor and sentiment that really reflected my husband as a person.

Family portraits can include all the family members, even those with four legs. Just make sure there's someone on hand to take care of your furry friends after the photo op so you can enjoy the party.

INGRID: A blessed memory.

For me, it was my father's blessing before the meal at the reception. In it, he quoted a poem written by my mother, who had passed away several years before. It made her present at a moment when I missed her very much.

What did you do to pamper yourself before the wedding?

ERICA: Perfect hair.

I had my hair blown out three days in a row. What a treat!

CINDY: Dream dress.

I bought the dress I wanted, despite the fact that it was priced a little higher than I anticipated. It was worth it. I was confident, and I felt great in that dress. It shaped my attitude for the entire day.

KATE: Glowing skin.

I scheduled facials for six months prior to the wedding. It was wonderful and my skin looked so good! I also did a few trials with professional spray-tanning to achieve a natural-looking glow for my wedding day.

LINDSAY: A place of her own.

I rented a suite at a hotel so that my bridesmaids and family could hang out while we all got ready. Nothing like a good iPod mix, some bubbly, and your best friends to keep you stress-free on the big day!

DANA: A bridal assistant.

I indulged by hiring a personal assistant for the weekend, provided by my wedding planner. She helped keep me on time, packed gift bags for my guests, and located my missing accessories. She also tackled many other important tasks.

KATIE: Red-carpet styling.

We had hair and makeup artists come to my hotel room to style me, the bridesmaids, and a few family members. It was so nice to be able to spend the hours leading up to the big event with those closest to me.

LESLEY: Setting boundaries.

My regular work hours can extend into the evening with meetings and tasks. However, I decided that during the two weeks prior to the wedding, I wouldn't participate in any work-related meetings that were outside of the regular nine-to-five workday. It was a welcome splurge to get home at a decent time each evening to work on wedding tasks or just relax with my husband-to-be.

Share any gown details, such as a bustle or complicated fasteners, with your maid of honor or a friend who can help you into your dress when you might be nervous and excited.

Do you have any advice for other brides about hair, makeup, the dress, or accessories?

DEBBY: Go to trial.

Spend the money for professional makeup, and do advance trials—even if they are an additional expense. Getting your look just right is worth it.

CINDY: Fake it.

I bought a piece of faux hair that was added to my updo to make my hair look fuller. You cannot tell the difference in the pictures between my real hair and the fake hair, and it felt totally natural.

KATE: Your hair, your way.

I was being pressured by friends, parents, and seemingly everyone, to have an updo. I insisted on having my own style and I wore my hair partially up. My husband loved it, I looked like myself (but better and more polished), and I felt beautiful. I know that when I look at my wedding pictures years from now, I will not regret that decision.

JENNIFER: Accentuate the positive.

I recommend finding a professional makeup artist who can play up your best features while correcting your less-favored features. My artist did a terrific job emphasizing my eyes (my favorite feature) and making my skin (my least favorite feature) look flawless.

What did you worry about most before the wedding?

ERICA: A rainy day.

I worried about the weather—a complete waste of time!

DEBBY: Are we having fun yet?

I worried whether people would have fun at the wedding.

CINDY: Play nice.

Whether or not my family would behave.

KATE: The best laid plans . . .

I worried incessantly about the weather. I freaked out when, two weeks before the wedding, the forecast called for cold and rain. After spending 16 months envisioning my summer garden wedding, and planning and controlling each and every detail, the weather was the only thing I could not control, and I was devastated by the idea that the weather could be anything less than perfect.

I also worried a lot about making sure that everything was totally, completely, 100% organized. I had a giant spreadsheet, which I included in our welcome baskets for everyone who was in our wedding, telling them exactly where to be and when. In hindsight, I think that I could have let the weekend take on a more natural flow, rather than dictating every minute of every single person's time, and things would have turned out fine.

DANA: Will they dance?

I worried whether everyone would be up and dancing and having a great time at the reception. We chose a fun, upbeat song for the bridal-party entrance, which set the tone for the whole party. I think the only time people moved off the dance floor was during the main course.

KATIE: Mirror image.

I worried about losing weight and looking good. I wasted so much time worrying about all of the superficial stuff!

LESLEY: Musical chairs.

We had a big wedding, and managing the RSVPs became a major task. I was worried about people who replied not coming and the prospect that people who were designated to come alone might bring a date. I started imagining both empty reception tables and guests standing around without seats. Of course it all worked out perfectly.

INGRID: Family matters.

The most stressful parts of the wedding were juggling family politics and making people feel included, while having the event reflect our preferences. We turned down an offer to have an artist in the family make our invitations and asked that she instead do two larger pieces that we put on easels leading into the reception. It worked out beautifully.

Did you forgo anything for the wedding that you now wish you had splurged for or included?

DEBBY: A good point-person.

We should've spent the money on a really good coordinator for the wedding day. I hired someone, but that was one of my on-the-cheap decisions that didn't work out so well.

DANA: Not a thing.

We had a few ideas come up at the last minute, which I'm glad that we skipped. Looking back, those last-minute additions were not worth the extra time or money. If you didn't want them in the previous months of wedding planning, you probably won't miss them when they are not there on the big day.

INGRID: Speech!

Opportunities for people to give toasts. Our welcome dinner on Friday was very casual, and there was no sound-system available, nor any specific moment allotted for people to speak. We found out afterward that people wanted to say something but didn't find the opportunity. If I could do it again, I would organize this detail a little better.

JOY: Holiday right away.

I wish we could have left for the honeymoon right away instead of going back to work. There is an indescribable high from the wedding that a couple should continue by having a holiday.

acknowledgments

First and foremost, I'd like to thank all the brides I've had the pleasure to know and work with. You've taught me so much, and you've invited me into a very special part of your lives. I will always be grateful to each and every one of you.

Next, I am lucky enough to know a lot of smart people, and I'm also lucky that they agreed to help me with expert advice throughout this book. Thank you, Sean Green, Beth Chapman, Jacqui Phillips, Vincent Roppatte, for taking the time to share your expert advice and great tips to help brides navigate their way to the big day with more style and less stress.

For this book, I asked some of the country's best wedding photographers to contribute images to inspire our readers. Sabine Scherer, thank you for shooting the cover photograph and so many of the other beautiful images within these pages. Mel Barlow, Christian Oth, Brian Dorsey, Jenson Sutta, Belathée, Cappy Hotchkiss, Steve DePino, Carla Ten Eyck, Virginie Blachère, and Lawrence Jenkins, thank you all for helping to make these pages come alive with your beautiful work. Kelley Marks, thank you so much for being a total trooper on a freezing day, and for gracing our cover (and numerous pages) with your bridal beauty. Thanks to the wonderful staff at The White Dress for their help and hospitality. Big thanks also to Christine Toner of Stonington Paperie and Linnea Rufo, *innkeeperista* at the Bee & Thistle.

As always, I am indebted to Leslie Stoker and Jennifer Levesque at Stewart, Tabori & Chang. I am overwhelmed by your kindness and so thankful for your guidance and support. Joy Tutela, thank you for believing in me, and for introducing me to more incredible people than I would have ever dreamed possible.

One of those incredible people is my manager, Marianne Hayden. Thank you, Marianne, for all you do to spread the Simple Stunning message, and for helping to keep the whole team jazzed up and on track on our journey toward the wonderful things to come.

James Gregorio, thank you for your ever-wise counsel. Chris Tsamutalis and Dana Lucas, thank you both so much for being brilliant.

Susi Oberhelman is our super-talented book designer. She puts words and pictures together to create magic. Susi, to put it in the simple stunningest terms possible, "You rock."

Hey, Danielle Burch, you're fabulous! Hey, Sarah Hall, you're awesome! Thanks to you and to your whole team for making me look good.

Finally, a big thank-you goes out to my whole team, especially Nicole Fazzini and Tom Cawley. You inspire me every day.

resource guide

Photographers

Some of my favorite photographers submitted images for this book. You can find the specific page credits on the copyright page. Check out their fabulous websites for contact info and more details.

www.sabinescherer.com
www.briandorseystudios.com
www.melbarlow.com
www.christianoth.com
www.cappyhotchkiss.com
www.jensensutta.com
www.stevedepino.com
www.carlateneyck.com
www.virginieblachere.com
www.lawrencejenkinsphotography.com

index